Note for Librarians: A cataloguing record for this book is available from Library and Archives Canada at www.collectionscanada.ca/amicus/index-e.html
ISBN 1-4251-0240-9
Grateful acknowledgment is made for permission to quotecopyrighted material:

Magical Worlds of the Wizard of Ads, Copyright© 2001, Roy H.Williams, reprinted by permission of Bard Press, Austin, TX,www.bardpress.com.

Hypnosis in Contemporary Medicine, Copyright© April 2005,Mayo Clinic Proceedings, James H. Stewart, M.D., Mayo ClinProc, 2005;80:511-526 with permission.

Printed in Victoria, BC, Canada. Printed on paper with minimum 30% recycled fibre. Trafford's print shop runs on "green energy" from solar, wind and other environmentally-friendly power sources.

TRAFFORD
PUBLISHING™

Offices in Canada, USA, Ireland and UK

Book sales for North America and international:
Trafford Publishing, 6E–2333 Government St.,
Victoria, BC V8T 4P4 CANADA
phone 250 383 6864 (toll-free 1 888 232 4444)
fax 250 383 6804; email to orders@trafford.com
Book sales in Europe:
Trafford Publishing (UK) Limited, 9 Park End Street, 2nd Floor
Oxford, UK OX1 1HH UNITED KINGDOM
phone 44 (0)1865 722 113 (local rate 0845 230 9601)
facsimile 44 (0)1865 722 868; info.uk@trafford.com
Order online at:
trafford.com/06-1997

10 9 8 7 6 5 4 3 2 1

DISCLAIMER

The Author Entities, hereinafter referred to as "AE's", are defined as, but not necessarily limited to, the author (Lynsi Eastburn), any Eastburn Hypnotherapy Center practice or location, any location of the Eastburn Institute of Hypnosis, all employees of any above author or entity, and any contractor, instructor, agent, heir, legal assign, or corporate sponsor of the above author or entity.

The AE's, offer the material printed in this book only as an informational study. None of the contents of this book may be considered formal advice. Such material is to be considered a guideline, to be reviewed and/or approved by your doctor(s), mental health professionals and/or other licensed medical providers. It is the responsibility of each person who purchases this book, and each person who may read or encounter the contained material, to comply with locally applicable laws, and to seek professional advice in any health-related matter.

No claims are made by the AE's as to the fitness of the contents of this book for any specific use. No form of warranty, expressed or implied, is offered to any reader of this book, regardless of whether or not said reader is the original purchaser of the book. The accuracy and relevance of the material contained in this book are not guaranteed in any way, expressed or implied. The AE's are not obligated to inform readers of any changes to facts presented in this book. By opening this book, all readers agree to recognize that the facts in the covered subject matter will change periodically, and represent the opinions of those reasonably accepted to be experts in various fields, whose opinions may be subject to controversy and disagreement. Updates to the material are not an obligation of the AE's.

In addition, the AE's are not responsible for damages that result to any person or entity outside of those who have read this book, even if said damages occur as a result of the use of information herein.

All readers are held by the terms of this disclaimer, made binding by possessing this book and/or by being directly or indirectly exposed to any part of its content, whether in writing, verbally or through any other medium.

Should the AE's develop and offer any courses related to the material in this book, the above indemnity shall extend to such a course, whether or not said course uses this book as part of the course material, or is referenced in that course.

CONTENTS

CONTENTS (continued)

FOREWORD

Every day we hear of new medical breakthroughs as a result of a deepening scientific understanding of how the human body functions. While we often read in the media about the major technological advances in pharmaceuticals and surgical approaches, there has been a much quieter revolution taking place in how we understand the important interaction between mind and body. Thirty years ago when I graduated from Northwestern University Medical School there was no such thing as mind-body medicine. One either had a physical problem for which you saw a regular doctor, or it was all in your head in which case you were referred to a psychiatrist. There was no language in which to speak about the effects of the emotions on the body or vice-versa, let alone a scientific understanding of the anatomy and biochemical pathways in the brain and elsewhere that underlie the mind-body connection.

However, today, in light of a tremendous wealth of recent research in the last thirty years, our conception of the human body is rapidly changing. We now know that the roughly two hundred trillion cells in our body are in constant communication with each other primarily through biochemical messenger molecules known as neuropeptides — small proteins secreted from neurons and other cells, which traditionally were referred to as hormones. These neuropeptides, which now number over a hundred, control everything from thirst and hunger, to ovulation and menstruation, to the regulation of our activity level and emotional mood. With the discovery of neuropeptides and their anatomical location in the brain we have identified an important anatomical and biochemical basis by which the mind communicates with the body.

At the same time this research confirms what people have

intuited throughout the ages — that mental phenomena have a physical effect on the body. At a phenomenological level the mind and body always come together as a single package. People who are chronically worried and stressed out are more apt to get sick and conversely physical illnesses can profoundly affect our emotional mood. We know quite well that by altering our biochemistry with certain drugs we can affect our mental state. Anti-anxiety drugs and more recently anti-depressant drugs have been widely used. But it is a two-way street. If we see an enjoyable movie and afterwards walk out of the theater with a smile on our lips and a lightness in our step, we must conclude that the movie has changed our biochemistry at a cellular level.

It is really not surprising then that a growing body of research has demonstrated that fertility rates can be significantly improved through mind-body techniques such as hypnosis. The entire process from initial sexual attraction, to conception, to delivery is a highly complex chain of events that is regulated by neuropeptides from beginning to end.

Although we are accustomed to viewing our body in medical terms as a complex biochemical machine, the creation of new life goes far beyond our scientific understanding into the realm of deep mystery. To stand at the edge of this mystery is one of the most exhilarating and sacred of all human experiences. In this sense conception and childbirth represents the fruit of human life. And as with a fruit tree, should there be a problem anywhere from the stem to the root — from the moisture in the air, to the nutrients in the soil — it is the fruit that will be the first to fall.

Our body is so much more than a piece of equipment with replaceable parts. This is all the more true when it comes to the issue of fertility. My advice, as a physician who has practiced mind-body medicine for many years, is to first approach the sacred mystery of fertility with humility and hope as countless generations of women and men have throughout time. I believe that this splendid book Lynsi Eastburn has written will help you re-integrate mind with body and greatly assist you in your journey to parenthood.

— Jia Gottlieb, M.D.

American Board Family Practice
NCCA Certified Acupuncturist
Still Mountain Clinic, Boulder, CO

"I live for my sons. I would be lost without them."

— Princess Diana

This book was inspired in many ways by my two wonderful sons, Kel and Dylan. As I write this they are 16 and 11 years old. I love being a mother, and am particularly grateful to be their mother. They are bright, creative, sensitive, kind, friendly . . . the list is endless. The sheer force of the love I feel for these young men is incredible. Although I have accomplished many things in my life, it is in being their mother that I am the most satisfied, the most fulfilled.

I have encountered many people who have little interest in children, people who believe that the conception of any child could only have been by accident. I have heard people say that there are enough children in the world, so why waste time and energy on the creation of more? I don't agree with that. In fact, I strongly disagree. I believe there is always room for a wanted child, and I believe that ultimately all children are wanted, perhaps not always by their birth parents, but certainly by the Ultimate Universal Creative force which expresses them into existence.

It is in the faces of my boys that I am ever reminded of the gift that is motherhood. Not a single day goes by when I do not thank God for the privilege of knowing them and loving them, let alone being able to raise them and guide them. And with this privilege comes recognition and responsibility. I recognize that many people have not yet experienced the joy that comes of having a child. I realize that I have an inner knowing, and an ability to assist others in achieving their dreams, and therefore a responsibility.

I have a stepdaughter, Candace, and a stepson, Coady, from my first marriage. They are 22 and 20 years old now and although I am no longer married to their father, they have always remained close to me. Candace and Coady have shown more maturity in their lives than most adults could ever hope to and I have learned much from these children over the years. Though they are not of my flesh and blood, I love them completely. And because of them, I know firsthand that those you are to love in life will not always enter by "conventional" means. But it's worth it to be open and receptive.

My husband, Drake, is not only a gifted hypnotherapist, but a man of exemplary nature. Never having had any children of his own, he welcomed not only my boys, but also my stepchildren with a warm and loving heart. He is adored by all of us. And he is yet another inspiration to me as I journey through this lifetime.

I share my blessings with you so that you may know how dedicated I am to the purpose of assisting in fostering the parenting experience in whatever way possible.

Lynsi Eastburn
Arvada, CO
May 29, 2006

"People usually consider walking on water or in thin air a miracle. But I think the real miracle is not to walk either on water or in thin air, but to walk on earth. Every day we are engaged in a miracle which we don't even recognize: a blue sky, white clouds, green leaves, the black, curious eyes of a child — our own two eyes. All is a miracle."

— *Thich Nhat Hanh*

ACKNOWLEDGMENTS

This book would not have been possible without the assistance and support of Martie O'Brien, best known around Eastburn Hypnotherapy Center as the *Office Goddess*. Certified as a hypnotherapist, herself, Martie's many talents include editing and graphic design. She thoroughly enjoys personal interaction with the Center's many clients and students, and her warmth and sincerity are greatly appreciated by all. Martie's unique combination of soothing voice, compassion, and kindness has often been referred to as a balm for the soul, and she is truly inspirational in her ability to honor her life purpose every day.

I'd also like to thank:

Barb Lundy for her quick and efficient editing skills and assistance.

Mary Casey for her support and assistance, including — but definitely not limited to — editing.

Philo Couch *A.K.A. the Computer Wizard* for the cover design, body layout, endless hours of production assistance, editing, attention to detail . . . and much more.

Amber Olson for contributing the cover photo of her

adorable son, her willingness to share her story for the benefit of others, and for her professionalism, positive energy and the compassion she brings to our office.

Jennifer Harris for contributing the *I'm gonna be a big sister* back cover photo of her beautiful daughter, her willingness to share her story to inspire others, and all the ways she supports women in their desires to have a family.

My original hypnotherapy instructor and mentor, Arthur Leidecker, for his magnificent teaching style and thorough training, and his generous assistance and encouragement every step of the way, including some editing assistance with this book.

Dr. C. Scot Giles for believing in me right from the moment we met, for mentoring me, for teaching me some of the most profound advanced hypnotism techniques, and for his endless support and encouragement.

Marie "Mickey" Mongan for immediately recognizing the value and embracing the proposal of the *Certified HypnoBirthing® Fertility Therapist* program.

Dr. Jia Gottlieb of Boulder's *Still Mountain* for his holistic approach to medicine and his support of me personally, my clients, and my work with hypnosis.

Dr. Jon Shick for his wholehearted acceptance of my

work and endless stream of patient referrals.

Dr. Mark Bush of Colorado's *Conceptions Reproductive Associates* for his open-mindedness and acceptance of the value of hypnosis to support fertility issues.

Dr. Jan Winetz, Dr. Gerald Trobough, and Certified Hypnotherapist Roxanne Paolini of the *Integrative and Wellness Medical Center of Silicon Valley* in Los Gatos for hosting my fertility training at their wonderfully progressive holistic fertility clinic.

The National Guild of Hypnotists for recognition and support not only of my fertility hypnosis work but also for their tireless promotion of hypnosis as a separate and distinct profession, and the ethical practice of hypnotism.

And especially my father, Garry Carter, whose sudden and tragic death less than two weeks after I learned I was pregnant with my eldest son prompted me to pursue mastery of the healing arts including meditation and hypnosis.

"Before you were conceived I wanted you.
Before you were born I loved you.
Before you were here an hour I would die for you.
This is the miracle of life."

— *Maureen Hawkins*

SPONSORS

The following people are talented hypnotherapists who have graciously supported my work and in sponsoring the book were instrumental in its completion.

Karen Riley, BSc, DHyp, BSCH, NAPCH, HBCE
HypnoBirthing® and HypnoFertility™ Yorkshire
The Astwood Clinic
22 New Hey Road
Huddersfield, West Yorkshire
HD3 3FD, UK
Telephone: 01422 373321
www.hypnofertilityyorkshire.co.uk

Karen Riley is a Registered Clinical Hypnotherapist specializing in hypnosis for conception, pregnancy and birth. Karen works with couples undergoing fertility treatments and has close links with several assisted conception units in the North of England. The author of the "IVF Companion" a hypnosis program for couples undergoing IVF treatment, Karen also speaks regularly to patients groups and medical staff about the use of hypnosis in combination with fertility treatments and unexplained infertility.

Sherry Gilbert
Healing & Transforming Lives
www.healinglives.net
www.healinglivescoaching.com
602.615.6445

Sherry Gilbert is a Certified Hypnotherapist, Life Coach, Certified HypnoBirthing® Educator and Hypnotherapy Instructor. She has additional certifications in Fertility Therapy and Smoking Cessation. Sherry is a member of the National Guild of Hypnotists. Her practice encompasses fertility, birthing, and re-birthing; as well as other standard hypnosis practices.

Richard Ferrell
Utopia Hypnosis
800 W. 5th Ave, Suite 106-B
Naperville, Illinois 60563-4944
Telephone: 630.420.8422

Richard M. Ferrell is a Certified Hypnotherapist with the National Guild of Hypnotists. He is certified through the HypnoBirthing® Institute as a Certified HypnoBirthing® Fertility Therapist, as well as being certified in Complementary Medical Hypnotism. Rich has trained and been certified in Innovative Hypnotic Techniques. He is the director of Utopia Hypnosis where he assists clients with fertility issues and also runs a general private hypnotherapy practice.

Desirae Manering
Pregnancy Birth and Beyond
Denver, CO
303.377.4791 or Desiraempregnantbirth.com

Desirae's education and training began in 1999 when she found her passion and desire to connect with women before, during and after pregnancy. She is a Certified Massage Therapist, Certified Hypnotherapist, has extensive training in Prenatal and Infant Massage Therapy, is a certified HypnoBirthing® Practitioner and Fertility Hypnotherapist. She trained with Lynsi Eastburn, the founder and creator of Hypnotherapy for Fertility. Desirae has also been a birth assistant (Doula) to more than 150 women. Combining all of these modalities, Desirae has created Pregnancy, Birth and Beyond, a successful practice in Denver dedicated to supporting women and their families through this important time in their lives. She works with women from the very beginning of their pregnancy through their childbirth. Her training in women's healing has taken her to Belize where she has studied ancient Maya Abdominal massage and healing techniques to support the reproductive health of women.

Kayla Wentworth
Life Force Wellness Center
360.598.3867
wapaske@earthlink.net
to reach me in England: 07973-111-552
www.hypnosis-reiki.com

Kayla is diverse in many practices. The body/mind/spirit

is the curricula in which she is an international teacher and a guide as she passes living wisdom to others. Kayla is a Certified Clinical Hypnotherapist, Yoga and Meditation Instructor, Nutritionist, Herbalist, and is a Certified HypnoBirthing® Practitioner and Fertility Therapist. She has a private hypnotherapy practice and teaches HypnoBirthing® classes in Poulsbo, WA and in England. Kayla's goal is to help women to conceive naturally and to provide support through the entire fertility process, assisting her clients in attaining personal empowerment for optimum health and well being.

Nicolett Katz, CH, HBCE, CMT, Core Energetics Therapist
www.boulderwellnesscenter.com
303.378.6570

Nicolett keeps an active practice in Boulder, CO. Her background is in nursing, massage therapy, Core Energetics (body psychotherapy) labor support, HypnoBirthing® and hypnotherapy. Due to her various trainings she is able to blend techniques and modalities to help support the evolution of each client. Her focus is on fertility, stress management and related health concerns, smoking cessation, anxiety, and hypnosis for childbirth. Nicolett's main concern and focus are client oriented methods to achieve maximum and lasting results. It is her passion to work with women and women's issues and to offer support through many years of working with women in her practice.

Lea Blumberg
480.502.5074
www.newlifeawareness.com.
E-mail: info@newlifeawareness.com.

Lea is the director of New Life Awareness Institute and is a certified hypnotherapist who specializes in women's issues. She holds certifications in Medical Hypnosis, Fertility Therapy, Prenatal Parenting®, HypnoBirthing®, Professional Labor Assistance, Smoking Cessation, Weight Loss Management, NLP, and Time Line Therapy®. She has had special training in Cancer and related issues, Pain Management, Environmental Illness, Hospice, and Past Life Regression. She is registered and certified through the National Guild of Hypnotists, National Federation of Neuro-Linguistic Psychology, Time Line Therapy Assoc., HypnoBirthing® Institute, and Arizona Society for Professional Hypnosis. Lea is also the director of the Prenatal Parenting Program for the state of Arizona where she has been studying and practicing since 1986.

Martie O'Brien, CH, CHFT
7768 Vance Drive
Arvada, CO 80003
303.424.2331
martie@hypnodenver.com

Martie O'Brien is a Certified Hypnotherapist and Certified HypnoBirthing® Fertility Therapist. She is an assistant instructor at Eastburn Institute of Hypnosis and office manager of Eastburn Hypnotherapy Center. Martie has a general hypnotherapy practice in Arvada and Florence, CO, with an emphasis on transpersonal work.

Deanna Figueiredo
130 Harbord Street
Toronto, Ontario M5S 1G8 Canada
416.486.8246 ext. 300
deannamf@hotmail.com

Deanna Figueiredo M.S.W., R.S.W. is a clinical social worker, psychotherapist and a NGH certified hypnotherapist with a private practice in Toronto, Canada. She holds a Bachelor's degree in Psychology and a Master's degree in Social Work. Deanna has many years of experience counselling adults, children, adolescents and families. In her private practice, her areas of expertise include depression, anxiety, grief and bereavement, self-esteem issues and relationship conflict. She works with people to help improve relationships and gain insight into past events and present difficulties, as well as learn positive ways to cope with life's challenges. Deanna is particularly interested in working with women who are experiencing infertility. She follows the unique HypnoFertility™ program developed by Lynsi Eastburn to help women conceive. As a certified yoga teacher and hypnotherapist she has a special interest in helping people develop a mind-body awareness and connection.

"Making the decision to have a child — it's momentous. It is to decide forever to have your heart go walking outside your body."
— *Elizabeth Stone*

INTRODUCTION

If you've been drawn to this book, you probably feel you know more about pregnancy and infertility than most practicing medical specialists. Chances are you cry each time someone tells you they're pregnant and you avoid baby showers at all costs. You wonder, "What's wrong with me? Why can't I have a baby?" You've changed your diet—you don't drink, smoke or consume caffeine. You've even tried wheatgrass. You monitor your cervical mucous and meticulously track your menstrual cycles. You're hyper-sensitive to every twinge in your body. You feel like you should own stock in the companies that make ovulation kits and home pregnancy tests.

The tumultuous roller coaster that is now your life has dropped you deep into despair and you're not even sure why. It all started one day . . . you and your partner excitedly decided to start "trying." It was fun at first, romantic even, but then each month the start of your period would dash your excitement and before long the worry began to set in. Before you knew it you were so preoccupied with thoughts of conception that it was all you wanted to talk about. There's a strain on your relationship now, barely perceptible, perhaps, but there.

Well-meaning but sometimes insensitive advice of

friends or family has begun to wear on your nerves. And some of your friends will no longer look you in the eye. They stop talking when you enter a room and you know that they're talking about you. They feel sorry for you, or they think you're overreacting. That if only you'd relax you wouldn't have this problem.

You set up an appointment with your doctor, and she tells you not to worry about it. Focus on other areas of your life and let nature take its course. It's too soon to see a specialist. But as time goes on even the doctor begins to become concerned. You've *Googled* infertility — and found that you have a number of symptoms and that it is definitely possible that you could have any of these problems. You decide it's time to see a specialist.

You check with your insurance company to find out what infertility procedures they will cover — if any. One of the reproductive endocrinology practices you contact immediately runs a credit check on you, before you are even allowed to book a consultation. The reality of this process sets in, and what you've been through thus far is nothing compared to what is to come.

An infertility diagnosis in either partner answers some questions, but you were ill-prepared for the emotional impact. Terrible guilt for the afflicted party perhaps. Anger, rage, devastation, fear . . . depending on the diagnosis and the medical options.

Financial concerns and considerations . . . choices. It wasn't supposed to be like this.

For those whose diagnoses are medically treatable there are protocols that must be followed which can be time-consuming, painful, and expensive. And the statistics are not all that great. Although a diagnosis of "unexplained infertility" may seem positive to some, to others it is perceived as a terrible blow: if there's nothing physiologically wrong — there's nothing they can do. However, from a hypnosis standpoint there's a lot we can do — in either case.

I am a Board Certified Hypnotherapist and Instructor through the National Guild of Hypnotists, and have been working with hypnosis to promote fertility for several years. I have created a specialized program which utilizes the most powerful hypnosis techniques available for fertility and I have taught this program to therapists internationally. This book is based on my firsthand experience with clients and details the hypnotic process for your understanding.

Wherever you are in your fertility journey, if you've been guided to this book know that there is hope for you. As you read the client cases contained within you'll see how others have had successful pregnancies, sometimes despite unbelievable odds and in catastrophic circumstances. Hypnosis is a powerful adjunct to Assisted Reproductive Technology (ART), or to facilitate natural conception. At the Eastburn

Hypnotherapy Center we NEVER say never!

A recent Israeli study conducted by Professor Eliahu Levitas showed that the success rate of IVF treatments doubled when the subjects underwent hypnosis during implantation. Another study in the journal Fertility and Sterility *suggests that because mind/body programs are effective for reducing negative emotions that may impair IVF success, patients should be offered such a program in conjunction with IVF.*

One study by Dr. Alice Domar, published in 2000 in the journal Fertility and Sterility *showed 55% of the previously infertile women who met regularly in a mind/body program conceived, compared with 20% of the control group who used no mind/body techniques and who did not attend meetings.*

For further information including articles and research visit us on the web:

www.hypnofertility.com

"Bitter are the tears of a child: Sweeten them.
Deep are the thoughts of a child: Quiet them.
Sharp is the grief of a child: Take it from him.
Soft is the heart of a child: Do not harden it."

— *Pamela Glenconner*

Chapter 1
Beginning To Understand

"You gain strength, courage and confidence by every experience in which you really stop to look fear in the face. You are able to say to yourself, 'I have lived through this horror. I can take the next thing that comes along.' You must do the thing you think you cannot do."

— *Eleanor Roosevelt*

Chances are if you've been struggling with infertility issues you've been told to "just relax." And that has probably driven you crazy. In fact, you are probably tired of hearing those words; tired of people's insensitive, unwanted advice; tired of feeling out of control of your life. Hypnosis can help. Throughout this book I will use words you may have heard many times before: infertility; relax; think positive; stress; obsession; unexplained . . . and many others. From a hypnotic standpoint you will find that words often take on a different meaning or interpretation — and you must learn to speak (and think) from a hypnotic standpoint. As you begin to integrate hypnotic languaging techniques you will find it quite amazing that words which once elicited a terrible, gut-wrenching response from you are now processed smoothly and effectively, while you remain calm and in control of yourself and your life.

Due to misunderstandings surrounding the word "hypnosis" you will find that some references to it have been disguised by terms such as "guided imagery," "creative visualization," or simply "mind/ body" or "relaxation" techniques. These modalities do, in fact, stem from hypnosis, however, hypnosis is much more than simple guided imagery or visualization techniques. My skills in the use of hypnotism, including specialized inductions, and advanced suggestion application, increase the potency of the fertility work I do above and beyond that which a single-faceted technique can possibly achieve. This is crucial information for those of you who need to ensure receipt of the most powerful techniques available. This can be and often is the difference between success and failure.

I have elected to deliberately refer to my work as hypnosis as I feel it denotes the power not available in diluted versions of the practice. I refer to my work as hypnosis for fertility or HypnoFertility™. Graduates of my program are certified through the HypnoBirthing® Institute as Certified HypnoBirthing® Fertility Therapists. Though it is possible for anyone to use hypnotic suggestion to work with fertility issues, the methods illustrated in these pages are based on my program which I created after years of working one-on-one with fertility clients in my own private practice. Since the implementation of my certification program in 2003, I have trained approximately 200 Certified HypnoBirthing® Fertility Therapists worldwide.

Throughout my years in private practice I commonly encountered women who had initially sought out my hypnotherapy services because their fear of needles was often aggravated or intensified by the infertility procedures they had undergone or would need to undergo. Experiencing such a deep state of relaxation (pretty much a foreign concept for a woman dealing with traditional "infertility") during the hypnotherapy session, these clients elected time and again to continue the hypnotherapy sessions to support the medical processes — and a new specialty was born.

Having had such a positive experience with hypnosis for their fertility issues, many of these clients then continued on with me to complete the Hypno-Birthing® process (a technique developed by Marie Mongan nearly two decades ago to facilitate an easier, gentler birthing that most mirrors nature). It seemed that the more little round headed pictures I accumulated, the more sense it made to create a Hypnotherapy for Fertility training program as a natural adjunct for Certified Hypnotherapists, especially those already practicing HypnoBirthing®.

My work with hypnosis for fertility is not opposed to conventional medicine. I work with women and/or couples to assist them in conceiving naturally or as an adjunct to Assisted Reproductive Technology (ART). The focus is not my concern; my goal is to help you to realize your dream: a healthy baby.

Chapter 2
Positive Words Create Positive Outcomes

"Do not anticipate trouble, or worry about what may never happen. Keep in the sunlight."

— *Benjamin Franklin*

Let's start with "infertility." This word itself is anti-hypnotic (negative) and therefore we will instead refer to "fertility" here. The subconscious mind is literal. You are the sum total of all that you repeat to yourself in the privacy of your own mind — it is essential that you choose your thought carefully. Compounding suggestion and repetition are methods of affecting the subconscious mind. If you choose to think "infertile" rather than "fertile" you are literally reinforcing a hypnotic suggestion. The subconscious mind responds to emotion — what sort of emotion does the word "infertile" dredge up for you? Understanding what hypnotic suggestion is and understanding where it comes from can help you create positive environments in your own life.

There are many definitions of hypnosis. We hear terms such as relaxation, suggestibility, and hypnotizability. We may think in terms of clinical hypnosis, psychology, private practice. The most clear and concise definition of hypnosis I can give you is this: hypnosis is the bypass of the critical factor of the mind allowing access to the subconscious. Let's look at how this may be done. Using different types of hypnotic induction methods, a Certified Hypnotherapist in an office setting will guide you into the hypnotic state. Progressive relaxation (relaxing different parts of the body in succession) and guided imagery are probably the most familiar methods, however, there are many ways to induce hypnosis and it's important to note that one does not have to be relaxed for hypnosis to occur. The goal is to access the subconscious mind. After all, if it were possible to create the necessary change consciously we would have no infertility issues to speak of, and no need for this specialty work.

Each and every person who wishes to be hypnotized can be hypnotized under the right conditions. It is a fallacy that strong minded people cannot be hypnotized. In fact, strong minded people often have some of the greatest success. There are three requirements necessary for hypnosis to occur: a minimal level of intelligence, an ability to follow simple instructions, and a willingness to be hypnotized. No hypnotist can make you do anything against your will. If they could, the world would be run by power crazed hypnotists who would hardly have a need to maintain private practices working with smoking cessation, weight loss and fertility issues.

Hypnosis is a learned skill. Some are better at it initially, but anyone can improve with a little practice. The mind does not have to be quiet or still during the hypnotic state, which often makes hypnosis preferable to meditation for some people. Hypnosis is a participatory process. The hypnotherapist works with you during your session to create the most powerful session for you based on the information you provide, and the goals you desire to achieve.

While in reality all hypnosis is self-hypnosis, there are some issues for which simple self-hypnosis will be sufficient, and others that require the facilitation of a skilled hypnotherapist. A skilled hypnotherapist can help you to accomplish more in just a few sessions than people are often able to accomplish themselves throughout their entire lifetimes.

There are a few misconceptions about hypnosis which must be addressed so that you can understand and benefit from the process:

I might get stuck in hypnosis. Not so. Even if the hypnotherapist were to leave the building and forget about you completely, you would do one of two things: drift into a natural sleep for a few minutes or simply open your eyes and emerge.

My secrets will be revealed! Hypnosis is not a truth serum. You are always aware of the process and in control of what is said or not said at any time during the session.

I don't want anyone to control my mind! Hypnosis is a state of heightened awareness, a tool with which you can tap into the power of your own mind and create positive changes in your life. The protective critical factor of the mind ensures that your morals, values, and beliefs are kept intact, and allows only positive suggestions into the subconscious.

I don't think I can be hypnotized! What if I can't go under? "Go under" is a poor choice of words to describe the hypnotic state. During hypnosis you are not asleep or unconscious and, in fact, experience a state of heightened awareness. Relaxation goes along nicely with hypnosis but is not a requirement. Hypnosis can occur when standing, sitting, with eyes open or closed. There simply needs to be a willingness on your part to participate and by following the instructions of the hypnotherapist you will be able to benefit from hypnosis.

What if I fall asleep?! It makes no difference whether you "remain awake" or "fall asleep" during a hypnosis session. It is only the opinion of your conscious mind which really has no way to gauge the hypnotic state and therefore may "think" you have fallen asleep when you are simply benefiting from a relaxed state.

Will you make me cluck like a chicken? To this I often jokingly respond, "Only if you think it is therapeutically necessary...." It is a myth that people can be made to do things against their will; you will not do something during the hypnotic state that you would not do otherwise. Hypnosis simply affords you access to the more powerful part of your mind, the subconscious mind, where you can make changes that will benefit you. You are always in control.

My mind is too sharp to be hypnotized. Only weak-minded individuals can be hypnotized. Not true. A sharp mind is an asset in accessing and benefiting from the state of hypnosis. Different induction methods will benefit different learning styles or information processing abilities. A skilled hypnotherapist will help you utilize your individual style and intelligence level to benefit from hypnosis.

All hypnosis is technically self-hypnosis, with the Certified Hypnotherapist functioning as a guide. Self-hypnosis, like meditation, is a highly effective method for reducing stress and creating an inner calm, however, a skilled hypnotherapist trained as a Certified HypnoBirthing® Fertility Therapist is required to facilitate some of the deeper work outlined in this book. A normal state of consciousness, hypnosis can be defined as concentrated and directed daydreaming. Whereas the word sleep is sometimes used to describe the trance state, you are far from being asleep when in hypnosis. A person in hypnosis is aware of his/her surroundings in a detached sort of way and is more receptive to acceptable suggestions.

Can everyone be hypnotized? Yes. Can we prevent

it? Yes, provided we know it is happening. Can a hypnotist make you do something against your will? No. But, advertising oftentimes convinces us that something is for our own good, that we must have a certain something, that there is truth in a particular statement. Advertisers often trigger our emotions and tap into our hopes, fears, dreams to sell us cars, attract us to restaurants. Many media messages convince us we cannot have a baby. This is also hypnosis — these are also hypnotic suggestions. This book will teach you how to protect yourself from the media, advertisers, naysayers, medical personnel; in short, to "dehypnotize" yourself and take back control of your life.

Chapter 3
Hypnosis Helps You Use Your Whole Brain

"Any idea, plan, or purpose may be placed in the mind through repetition of thought."

— *Napoleon Hill*

To understand hypnosis, you need to be aware of how the conscious and subconscious minds function. The human brain is divided into two main sections: the left hemisphere (the conscious mind) which is logical, linear, analytical, rational, decision-making; and the right hemisphere (subconscious mind) which is intuitive, imaginative, emotional, non-thinking, goal-achieving, protective, irrational. I always joke that the conscious mind is the part that reads all the self-help books! It knows what we need to do, even how to do it. However, the conscious mind is the weaker part of the mind and when the two are in conflict will lose to subconscious programming if we don't also address it.

The left-brained view of the world is considered the scientific perspective, regardless of the fact that we cannot create anything with our left brains that we have not first imagined with our right. Thinking outside the box is an ability we need to develop if we desire to transcend the limits of so-called "reality" and create success. The subconscious mind — the more powerful part of your mind — responds to imagery, patterns, poetry, music, metaphor. The critical factor of the mind functions as a door or screen that protects information in the subconscious mind, whether it is positive or negative. To create change at the subconscious level one must bypass the critical factor; the most effective method to achieve this is through hypnosis.

Any form of startle or shock will instantly bypass the critical factor of the mind. Formal hypnotic induction by a Certified Hypnotherapist is designed to distract the conscious mind (bypass the critical factor) whereby bringing the subconscious to the forefront. During the hypnotic state there is a physiological change that occurs in the brain which basically balances the two hemispheres of the brain, strengthening communication pathways between them. This makes you more receptive to suggestion for change in the form of imagery, pictures, patterns, and emotion which the hypnotherapist creates based on information provided by you during an intake session. The hypnotherapist does not have control of your mind, and you will not concede to a suggestion that is against your will. It has been my experience, however, that a lot of the work I do in my office is actually more of a "dehypnotizing" process. The reason is that your critical factor may be bypassed often during daily life leaving your subconscious mind open to suggestion without your being aware of it. As a result, sometimes formidable subconscious blocks are created without our realizing it.

Fear is an excellent example of what I am talking about. When we are afraid, we revert back to our genetic programming. When the "fight or flight" response is triggered, critical thinking is bypassed and our instincts (unconscious) kick in. This is particularly discouraging for fertility because, number one, the reproductive system is not considered necessary for survival and therefore is one of the first to be neglected in favor of parts and systems of the body necessary to run or fight; and two, an experience or comment that shocks or startles us will immediately bypass the critical factor (hypnosis) and a follow up direct suggestion (such as, "you will never be able to get pregnant") is accepted by the subconscious mind. This is especially true if the suggestion is delivered by someone perceived to be in authority (such as a doctor) and/or with enough emotion, imagery, color (television) to cause an imprint.

The latest hype in the media is the rising number of infertile couples. We hear news reports, read articles, hear celebrity gossip, see commercials, watch television shows that continually reinforce the "fact" that it is becoming more and more difficult to conceive. (More hypnotic suggestions.) Reality shows and sit coms focus on the anguish of infertility, making jokes about the obsessive behaviors often associated with it. Since many women wait until their mid to late thirties before starting a family, there is a lot more time for them to receive negative pregnancy input which contributes to negative reinforcement.

At one time pregnancy was a natural experience. People worried about getting pregnant not about whether or not they could. In the past if a couple didn't conceive right away it was just assumed that it would happen eventually. These days women are rushing to infertility specialists if they don't conceive on the first "try," and the pressure is incredible. Not to say that there may not be something physically wrong, in which case medical technology is appreciated. Just as with birthing, though, we need to consider some type of balance. It's wonderful that medical technology has advanced to where babies and/or mothers are able to survive when they wouldn't have before, but overuse of invasive medical procedures indiscriminately has detracted from birth as a natural experience, and turned it into crisis. Our bodies know how to procreate and they know how to give birth. I believe this is why hypnosis has been so successful with fertility assistance — it facilitates the mind/body/spirit balance which is simply in harmony with nature.

The medical profession instantly considers pregnancy *high risk* if the woman is 35 years old or more. This term is an example of what we in the hypnosis profession call *painted words* and their effects can be devastating. Because the language of the subconscious mind is emotion, any words which elicit emotion will have a hypnotic effect. When a medical professional tells you that you are *high risk* it triggers a fear response which automatically bypasses your critical factor, driving in the suggestion. Subsequent suggestions then have direct access to the subconscious as the critical mind is actively wrestling with the shock triggered by the initial diagnosis. If a woman is not yet pregnant, but confides in her physician that she is now contemplating becoming pregnant, an insensitive comment (intentional or otherwise) can have a distressing effect. The subconscious mind is protective yet it is non-thinking. Should the literal subconscious interpret *high risk* to be too dangerous, it can instantaneously put up a roadblock to pregnancy. Fortunately, hypnosis can quickly and often easily reverse the effect.

Chapter 4
You Can Stop
Negative Thoughts

"Remember, no one can make you feel inferior without your consent."

— Eleanor Roosevelt

In the last chapter, I discussed the impact of words on the subconscious. We also experience this with advertising. There are even sales and marketing books that teach you ways to access the subconscious mind. Depending on your purpose you might find this intriguing or insulting. The important thing is to know that you are not simply at the mercy of these experiences. You can protect yourself with a simple thought stopping technique.

Becoming more mindful of your thought will make it easier for you to choose your state of mind. Upon hearing a negative thought or suggestion, simply say to yourself "stop" or "cancel" and imagine drawing a big, red "X" through the thought in your mind. Or, if you prefer, you can imagine an eraser or the delete key of a computer. The goal is to use emotion and imagery to communicate with the subconscious. I use this technique whenever I go to a doctor and they want my medical history. I cancel out any suggestions of cancer, heart disease, etc. projected onto me through discussion of parents, grandparents, etc. After all, if I have to accept predisposition to everything someone in my family has had I may as well write myself off right now. I prefer to cancel those suggestions and focus on suggestions for good health.

I have taught what I refer to as the "cancel" technique to thousands of people through seminars, classes and even in private session. It's an awesome technique that is a simple yet powerful way to redirect your thought. *As you think so shall you be.* This universal law is often referred to by world renowned speakers including Wayne Dyer and Deepak Chopra. Both of these gentlemen have recommended many versions of this exact thought stopping process and Dr. Dyer has gone to great lengths in numerous publications to expand on these principles. I highly recommend the practice of Wayne Dyer's *Japa* Meditation which you will find on CD in his book *Getting in the Gap*. His book *The Power of Intention* also contains a powerful testimonial from a couple who applied Japa to their "infertility" experience and became pregnant despite five years of infertility and countless failures.

"Do not wait for leaders; do it alone, person to person."
— Mother Teresa

Case Study:

Having experienced three miscarriages and a failed IVF cycle in the past year and a half, 40-year-old Charlene was none too happy to have to start over again. She hated needles and was terrified of having to redo the painful shots necessary for IVF. She also dreaded the side effects which she'd experienced as mood swings, hot flashes, and painful ovaries. She'd been diagnosed with unexplained infertility and felt her time was running out. A successful executive with a strong personality, she was determined to repeat the IVF until she became pregnant, but she was deathly afraid of needles and the stress was nearly intolerable.

Session #1

I regressed Charlene to the experience that caused her needle phobia. She accessed an experience in a doctor's office at the age of three which we determined to be the source of the problem (the initial sensitizing event). After reframing the experience Charlene felt empowered and liberated. Upon future pacing (imagining a positive scene in the future) she was happy to find that she wasn't at all bothered by needles and that she could imagine herself with several healthy babies.

Session #2

Charlene's second session focused on the healthy stimulation of her ovaries and production of viable eggs. Her doctor's goal was six to ten eggs. She happily reported she had experienced only the mildest symptoms from the hormone injections in the past week, no mood swings at all, and no more needle problems! After hypnotizing Charlene, I guided her through a fear release (a technique used to purge her subconscious mind of negative thoughts, beliefs, expectations) and then spent some time connecting her to a successful point of reference. For hypnotic purposes, connecting with a point of reference means tapping into a previous success and utilizing the positive emotion accessed therein. We used the metaphor of a blueprint to set a strong foundation for a successful pregnancy.

Session #3

Charlene reported that the doctor said all was going very well. There were more follicles than expected for Charlene's age. Even though she was living from one ultrasound to the next, Charlene was impressed that she was not uptight about it as she'd been previously. Hypnotic reinforcement reminded her body that it knew what to do — that all was well. Charlene went inside and embraced her ovaries, gave them a pep talk, and encouraged them to produce strong, healthy eggs.

Session #4

Charlene's retrieval was successful! The doctors had thought they might get nine eggs; they retrieved fifteen. Her mood was great, she had been practicing self-hypnosis and tapping into her subconscious, envisioning her womb as soft, inviting, full of life, and welcoming her babies. After a rapid induction (a hypnotic technique which produces trance in less than three minutes) I reinforced Charlene's positive experiences with positive suggestion. She connected with her inner nurse (see below) who assured her everything was ready and that she would take good care of the babies. I followed up with another fear release to address any residual fears of past miscarriages/disappointment.

Session #5

Charlene was thrilled to be five weeks pregnant! She was feeling good; a little tired which doctors had said was quite normal. She had continued with her stress reduction CD and visualizations at home. A rapid hypnosis induction was followed by an opportunity to check in with her inner nurse. Her nurse told her she worried too much, and advised her to check in more often and she'd feel better. Communicating with her body, Charlene visualized embryos as tiny babies seat belted into her uterus. She took a pleasant journey through the enchanted forest. There, Charlene relaxed in a healing pool of water and connected with her inner Goddess — her inner knowledge and wisdom. In her future pace she had given birth and was holding her healthy babies. It's all behind them now!

Charlene gave birth to triplets a few months later.

The *inner nurse* is a powerful technique during which the client enters her inner world where she meets with a being (sometimes a nurse, doctor, midwife, angel, guide, etc.) who resides in her uterus. This being represents her own inner knowing or intuition and he/she provides the client with great comfort over the upcoming days, weeks, months, empowering her to participate in her own experience. Many of my clients have emerged from hypnosis excitedly reporting that their inner assistant has assured them that everything is functioning properly, that they are not alone, that he/she is on the job. The incredible accuracy of the inner assistant really illustrates how strong our own inner knowing is, and how important it is to trust our feelings. Several clients and students with endometriosis have reported independently that when they checked in with their inner nurse/assistant he/she was scraping wallpaper and repainting the room (womb).

Remember: the subconscious mind responds to pictures, imagery, metaphor. Though it may seem a little silly (conscious mind judgment) this visualization is highly effective.

The "enchanted forest" is yet another metaphor. The client enters a specially prepared room in an enchanted castle and proceeds to soak in a healing pool. This is an excellent subconscious purge and a wonderful opportunity for self-confidence building suggestion. It is also another opportunity to connect with her inner voice or higher self, this time in the form of an Inner Goddess — a wise being who remains ever connected to the divine, never affected by stress, tension, life's daily demands . . .

"Have you seen any fairies lately, or have you allowed the harsher facts of life to dull your 'seeing eye?'"

— Laura Ingalls Wilder

Chapter 5
The Power Of The Mind

"For one who has controlled the mind, it is the best of friends, but for one who has failed to do so, it remains the greatest enemy."

— The Bhagavad Gita

Many women are experiencing "infertility" due to physiological issues. Hypnosis can help with these issues in many ways including stress reduction and direct application complementary to medical procedures. Subconscious blocks have often been shown to be the cause of "infertility" whether there is a physiological cause or not. Unresolved sexual

trauma, abortion, miscarriage, abusive relationships, fear of imitating someone else's parenting mistakes, sudden death or injury to a loved one, and history of mental or physical handicaps are just a few of the subconscious blocks I've encountered interfering with conception. The key is to remember that you may not have any idea that these or other experiences have so profoundly affected you. Having comforted a friend through a teenage abortion experience has been the culprit in my clinical experience, as has an uncomfortable early childhood encounter with a seriously physically and mentally challenged individual.

Most of the clients who come to me for hypnotherapy have already seen a physician, often having received the "unexplained infertility" diagnosis. Many of these women are undergoing acupuncture, and, as you may be aware, acupuncture is widely accepted for the treatment of infertility. In fact, many reproductive endocrinologists will refer their patients to an acupuncturist to complement the IVF process. Hypnosis is a powerful adjunct to acupuncture, and the combination of these methods can effectively accelerate the fertility process — whether natural or medically assisted.

Occasionally women will express concern about getting their hopes up. This again plays into the fear and negative thinking I mentioned earlier. It is possible that you will never conceive a baby, but it is also possible that you will. It is important at this stage to release negative thinking: fear of getting your hopes up is negative thinking. Each and every person on the planet is able to deal with devastation or disaster if they have to. But at this point you don't know that you have to. The subconscious mind does not distinguish between "fact" and "fantasy" and therefore, processes negative thinking about not becoming pregnant as effectively as not becoming pregnant. And once you've achieved balance of mind/body/spirit you may find you have a new perspective altogether.

I work with women one-on-one and/or with their partners. I also work with male fertility issues. I have sometimes found men to have subconscious blocks similar to those women experience. It's interesting to note that many men who, at the initial infertility workup, tested normal, will be found to have a low sperm count upon retesting a year later. In other words, the emotional strain and stress a couple endures during a year of infertility testing and medical procedures, appears to have serious impact on the ability to conceive, which adds insult to injury.

We often forget (or it never even occurs to us) that men may also have unresolved issues involving previous pregnancies or abortion. There are many scenarios which may have occurred causing his subconscious mind to put up a protective block which can interfere with conception. Perhaps he's been devastated by a previous partner having an abortion when he really wanted the child. He may be concerned with repeating abusive behavior stemming from his own childhood experience. In these cases, hypnotic resolution can affect conception just as it does when addressing issues of the female.

Hypnotic patter, like musical lyrics, affects some of the most primitive parts of the brain. Bypassing the critical factor in this manner, which is necessary to access the emotional, imaginative subconscious mind, a Certified HypnoBirthing® Fertility Therapist is able to assist with the release of subconscious blocks. Evocation of emotion is the means by which we communicate with the subconscious mind, and provides an effective method of bypassing the rational, analytical part of the mind. Although both sides of the brain are necessary to correctly interpret spoken words, access to the non-verbal right hemisphere is essential for successful hypnotic process. Though right brain language—metaphors, similes, juxtapositions, emotion, poetic device, hypnotic suggestion—may be considered nonsense by the left brain, the impact on the subconscious is apparent.

Because the subconscious mind responds to metaphor, often basic fear release techniques using metaphors like ripping pages out of a book, erasing a blackboard, and, erasing and/or editing video clips are enough to eliminate subconscious blocks. Sometimes, however, we need a stronger tactic. In these cases we use hypnotic regression. An experienced fertility hypnotherapist will be able to assist you in deciding which course of action is right for you.

Case Study:

Sarah was 37 years old when she came to see me. She had been diagnosed with secondary infertility. She'd had difficulty conceiving her first child five years before due to "unexplained infertility." This time, however, the tests had shown such poor egg quality that her reproductive endocrinologist had told her in no uncertain terms that she would never again conceive a baby.

Sarah was devastated. She desperately wanted a sibling for her daughter. She felt in her heart that she would have another baby, but intellectually she was sure she wouldn't. After all, the doctors had said it was impossible now. Totally conflicted, Sarah struggled with depression, anxiety, and insomnia. She could hardly breathe. Her marriage was suffering and the child she did have was clearly picking up on her mother's distress.

Sarah asked if I could help her. I told her I could, that I never say never, regardless of what others say. I couldn't promise her a baby, but with my hypnotherapeutic techniques, I could help her achieve the best state of mind/body conducive to pregnancy. My initial goal with Sarah wasn't for her to become pregnant — but rather to get her life back. She'd gotten her fight or flight switch jammed and was spiraling desperately downward, out of control.

Sarah committed to a series of six hypnotherapy sessions beginning that very day. We started with a fear release technique — invaluable in a situation like this. The subconscious mind must be purged of the negative emotions exacerbated in this case by invasive procedures and medical diagnoses.

Sarah: Session #1

The bulk of Sarah's first session was spent in my getting to know her and finding out the background of her specific experience. Highly charged, emotionally overwhelming, infertility diagnoses are as unique as they are similar. The initial session is often spent mostly with the client unburdening herself of the painful incidents leading up to her decision to seek out my assistance. This in itself created a sense of relief for Sarah. As with most women in her position, she had found herself feeling forced to keep her pain to herself, misunderstood by well-intentioned friends and family; besieged by their well-meaning if often insensitive advice.

After our initial intake I began the hypnosis session with Sarah using a mental confusion induction technique designed to engage the conscious mind rapidly and alleviate excessive stress. Within moments she was deeply relaxed and receptive to the hypnotic process which would eventually lead to the conception of her baby. Sarah's breathing became deeper and more rhythmic as she used the power of her mind to create a place of safety for herself, a peaceful place in her mind where she could go to rejuvenate herself. The importance of such a simple technique cannot be understated; women like Sarah experience such high levels of stress they often have exhausted their adrenal systems completely.

From her safe place we proceeded to a classic fear release piece, where Sarah utilized imagery and metaphor in the form of tearing pages from a book which allowed her to release negative experiences, thoughts, or beliefs consciously recognized or not. Before ending the session I guided Sarah forward to a future time (experienced in present tense) where she was healthy and happy. She excitedly reported (with delight, and in a surprised tone of voice) that she was holding her newborn baby. At the end of the session Sarah emerged from hypnosis feeling positive and hopeful. Her homework was to listen to a stress reduction CD I gave her to help reinforce the relaxed state she had achieved in my office and to prepare her for deeper work in future sessions.

Session #2

After a check-in period where Sarah and I talked about her time since I'd seen her last and how she had integrated the first session, we were ready to begin the hypnotic process. Thrilled that she had been feeling much better since the hypnosis session,

Sarah proclaimed that she was feeling nearly her-self again. She was talking to rather than shrieking at her husband; she was playing with her daughter again. I guided Sarah into trance with a rapid in-duction. Quickly accessing her safe and special place Sarah was soon ready to proceed further in the fer-tility process.

I suggested she do a body scan; this is done to see *what's what* in the body, specifically the reproduc-tive system. Imagining herself in a tiny form, Sarah found herself inside her uterus.

Lynsi: Find yourself now inside your uterus. Imag-ine what it looks like—experience your uterus not in the clinical sense, not like something you would find in a medical textbook—imagine a cozy, com-fortable room where your baby can relax and grow. What's it like? Perhaps it looks something like a nursery, painted in pleasing colors. Perhaps there's a crib, a rocking chair . . . that type of thing. Tell me what it's like.

Sarah: It's beautiful, so calm and comfortable. It's a pale blue, very soft and soothing.

L: Okay. Now, become aware of a presence there.

You may not have known this, but there is a tiny being living within your uterus. Perhaps male or female, this being is very wise and experienced in the ways of fertility, pregnancy, and birth. Highly skilled and knowledgeable, this wonderful being is completely on your side. You may experience this being to be some type of doctor, nurse or midwife, or perhaps a healer, an angel. Commune with this very special being now and know that he/she is there to assist you. He/she knows everything possible to help you create a healthy pregnancy and will handle all the details so you can relax and let things happen. This wise being can communicate with you by phone or fax, e-mail or snail mail, or simply through your intuition. You are more open to your intuition now. You trust yourself. You know what you need to do.

S: Yes. Her name is Diana. She is a strong female and she is telling me everything is all right. I will have my baby.

L: Become aware that there is a tiny car seat in your womb. When the time is right Diana will fasten your baby safely into the car seat and she will ensure your baby is secure. She will keep watch and notify you if there is anything you need to do. Is there anything you need to ask of Diana?

S: No, everything is fine. Diana knows exactly what she's doing.

L: All right, take a deep breath now and go deeper into hypnosis.

I followed this interactive piece with some positive confidence building suggestions based on information Sarah had given me earlier. Before concluding the session she progressed forward and experienced holding her baby once again. I added a second CD focused on self-esteem to Sarah's homework practice. She could now alternate between the two.

Session #3

Sarah reported that she was feeling stronger and much calmer. Her attitude was more positive. She had attended a baby shower for a friend and had felt good about it. She was relieved not to have felt jealousy or resentment, and had enjoyed shopping for the baby gift. Tapping into these positive points of reference I was able to weave ego strengthening suggestions that reinforced Sarah's confidence in her body's natural ability to conceive. By the time Sarah had completed four of the recommended six hypnosis sessions she was thrilled to discover she was naturally pregnant with her second child despite the "fact" that she would "never conceive another baby." She plans to wait until the birth of the baby to find out if her daughter will have a brother or sister.

Once pregnancy has occurred my clients often find it beneficial to continue with an occasional hypnosis session to reinforce a positive pregnancy and birth experience. This is a personal choice that I leave up to my clients. HypnoBirthing® *The Mongan Method* is often the preferred method of birthing and a natural follow-up to fertility hypnosis.

"Many persons have a wrong idea of what constitutes true happiness. It is not attained through self-gratification but through fidelity to a worthy purpose." — Helen Keller

Case Study:

Allison was 28 years old when she booked her first fertility session with me. She had a child from a first marriage but had been unable to get pregnant during the past four years with her second husband. Her doctor had diagnosed her with "unexplained infertility" which Allison found devastating. At least, by her way of thinking, if there was a physiological reason something could be done about it. There would be a medicine, a surgery, something that would remedy the situation. But unexplained? That meant there was absolutely nothing she could do; nothing the doctors could do.

Allison was depressed and frustrated. She had spent a lot of money and time trying to get pregnant. Sex had become a chore. The fertility drugs made her sick and she had gained a lot of weight. The IUI's were painful and she knew IVF would be worse — and even more expensive. She was about ready to give up on her dream of having another baby.

During the intake Allison told me she'd had an abortion since giving birth to her first child. Her husband had been abusive. He was a drug addict and didn't work. She could barely take care of her first child let alone have another one. She drove herself to the abortion clinic and tried to forget about it. But she hadn't forgotten — she'd just buried it in her subconscious.

During her first hypnosis session I assisted Allison in establishing a safe place. She accessed her inner nurse and made sure everything was ready for the baby. I gave her a stress reduction CD and instructed her to listen to it between the first and second session, when I would do a regression to resolve the abortion issue.

Session #2

I regressed Allison to the abortion experience. In trance her baby appeared before her.

Lynsi: What's happening?

Allison: My baby, my sweet baby is here. He is so serene. My baby is at peace. I'm so sorry. I'm sorry my baby. I didn't mean to hurt you. (Sobbing.)

L: Would you like to ask your baby for forgiveness? Not in the religious sense, but in a way that will release you from this terrible guilt?

A: Yes. He forgives me! He says it's all right. It was supposed to be this way. He says to forgive myself. He is okay. He is sending another baby to me. I'm not a bad person, he understands and it is okay. I'm holding him now. His heart against my heart. He is always with me.

L: Is there anything else at this time?

A: No, this issue is resolved.

L: Move forward in time now, a few months, a year or so. What's happening?

A: I am pregnant! I can feel my baby moving within me. Now, I've given birth—I'm holding my baby, he is healthy. He is beautiful.

About five months after Allison's second session she dropped in on a seminar I was giving to show me her pregnant belly. Her son was born with HypnoBirthing® less than a year after that first session, in early 2004.

Often during the hypnotic process, especially during regression, the word forgiveness will arise. I always stress to my clients that they may wish to forgive or ask forgiveness—not necessarily in the religious sense—but in a way that will release them from the bonds of guilt that enslave them. Due to misconceptions of the word forgiveness often stemming from prior religious experience, there is sometimes association with words like deserve and/or punish. I believe the greatest spiritual growth occurs as we learn to forgive—ourselves and others—without judgment.

IT'S CONCEIVABLE

"Come, come, whoever you are.

Wanderer, worshipper, lover of leaving — it doesn't matter.

Ours is not a caravan of despair.

Come, even if you have broken your vows a hundred times, a thousand times.

Come, come again, come."

— Rumi

Chapter 6
Overcoming Obstacles

"You see things; and you say, 'Why?' But I dream things that never were; and I say, 'Why not?'"

— *George Bernard Shaw*

Karen Riley is a hypnotherapist in the UK. She took my fertility training when I was in England in 2005. Recently, I received an e-mail from Karen updating me on the work she has been doing in the field of hypnosis for fertility. Karen has been working with two assisted conception units very closely and has herself developed a hypnosis program *The IVF*

Companion which has been working so well that the doctors at these units have made the decision that all new patients should be informed about hypnosis for IVF when they arrive for their first meeting to start their treatment. These doctors have asked Karen to attend these meetings and speak directly to their patients to let them know what it is all about. The following case was forwarded to me by Karen.

Karen Riley: I first met Lucy and Tom in July of 2005; they have been married for 12 years and are both 38 years old. Lucy is a human resources manager for a large firm and Tom is a university lecturer. They had been "trying" to conceive for four years and were on their fourth course of clomid out of a recommended six. The results of their medical tests had returned clear and they had received a diagnosis of primary unexplained infertility.

During the intake interview Lucy expressed that she felt that she was being punished for leaving it so late to start a family. She had a busy career and it had taken a lot of time for her to find a consultant who was willing to do an elective c-section because she had a phobia of childbirth. She also reported that she was an anxious person and, in fact, lived in terror that she would have to have any medical procedure. She had found the fertility investigations to

44

be harrowing, but was determined to become pregnant. As the interview progressed it became clear that her phobia was more about the pain of childbirth and the possibility of emergency interventions. Her mother had also informed her that her birth had been a difficult one, and that her brother's mental disability had been caused by oxygen deprivation during birth.

Over the course of six two-hour sessions we addressed her anxiety and her phobia through hypnotic desensitization, inner child work, and parts therapy. I taught Lucy self-hypnosis which she practiced between sessions. Future pacing from conception to several weeks past birth created a blueprint of success in Lucy's mind, and her confidence increased as her subconscious mind accepted that she could, in fact, have a successful pregnancy. Lucy and Tom are now expecting their first child in May 2006 and are planning to attend HypnoBirthing® classes for a more natural birth.

This classic mind-body phobic avoidance, where her body was subconsciously avoiding pregnancy, responded beautifully to the hypnotherapeutic techniques mentioned and Lucy became pregnant very quickly afterwards. Pregnancy occurred after the clomid treatment, before IUI.

Parts Therapy is a powerful technique during which the hypnotherapist facilitates a dialogue between conflicted parts of the personality. (This is not indicative of multiple personalities, we all have inner conflicts/parts such as the part who wants to get to work on time and the part who wants to sleep till noon, etc.) Resolution of the issue is accomplished through effective mediation of all parts concerned. An example of a need for Parts Therapy would be something like: "Part of me wants to get pregnant and part of me doesn't want all the responsibility involved with having a baby." During hypnotic trance the hypnotherapist would address any and all parts concerned, hearing them out without judgment and negotiating resolution.

Hypnosis for Inner Conflict Resolution: Introducing Parts Therapy *by Roy Hunter is an excellent resource. You may visit Roy's web site at: www.royhunter.com.*

Chapter 7
Hypnotic Regression Finds The Source Of The Problem

"Who controls the past controls the future: who controls the present controls the past."

— George Orwell

- ISE Initial Sensitizing Event
- SSE Subsequent Sensitizing Event
- SPE Symptom Producing Event
- SIE Symptom Intensifying Event

Should you decide on regression, your hypno-therapist will build what's called an affect bridge (the feeling technique) based on your most evident feelings. For example, some women will say that they feel frustrated about their fertility issues. Others may be sad, angry, impatient, apathetic, enraged, etc. Each client's experience is unique and I have no expectations as to which feelings they should have. Once I've determined the focus of the regression, I will typically use a rapid induction method and then using a five to one count, have my client follow the feelings back till we reach the initial sensitizing event, the first time the client experienced that feeling.

There are many techniques for inducing a hypnotic regression. The goal of the regression is for the client to travel back in time to an incident deemed to be the cause of their particular issue. For fertility purposes, the goal of the regression is to find the initial sensitizing event—the event which initially resulted in the subconscious mind finding it necessary to impose some type of protection mechanism which resulted in eventual "infertility." The symptom producing event or SPE, such as an unexplained infertility diagnosis or even blocked tubes or some other type of physical condition, is what typically lands the client in hypnotherapy. In our search for the initial sensitizing event (ISE) we will most likely encounter several subsequent sensitizing events or SSE's which I will explain here. I find it easiest to explain this process backwards.

Age regression (starting from the client's age and moving back in time) or calendar regression (starting from the present date and moving back) are techniques sometimes used for hypnotic regression. I prefer the affect bridge because it tends to engage the subconscious mind more effectively (emotion being the language of the subconscious mind) and it appeals less to the conscious mind (which easily interferes with a nice linear count backwards). I start from the symptom producing event and work toward the initial event that caused the block by following the presenting emotion back through time. I don't know how it might have been created until I have completed the uncovering process and arrived at the ISE. It's important to remember that the initial sensitizing event may not seem to be consciously related to the subsequent sensitizing events, however, due to "trance logic" or the function of the non-thinking subconscious mind, I deal with what emerges in the session and make no judgments.

Because suggestion is strengthened with repetition or compounding, there is actually a chain of events that occurs eventually leading to the fertility issue. The initial event almost always occurs before the age of 3 and is not usually consciously recognized. If a client comes in and says, "I want a regression, I had a teacher in the 7th grade whose baby died . . . ," that is most likely not the initial event, no matter how certain the client may be that it is. I will keep the information in mind and will make sure not to have an agenda either way as I work with the client. In my own private practice and teaching experience I have found this to be an effective guideline, and in comparing notes with some of the greatest regression hypnotherapists in the field I have found reports of similar experience.

Chapter 8
Releasing Subconscious Blocks

"With our thoughts we make the world."

— Buddha

Creating an affect bridge, or finding a key emotion that helps a client return to important moments in the past, is one of the hypnotherapist's most important strategies. An example of following an affect bridge may occur in this manner:

This begins after a thorough intake.

Client: I am devastated that I cannot have a baby. I feel that my life is incomplete. My husband is wonderful but I can hardly stand to look at him, I feel like such a failure.

Hypnotherapist chooses a client centered induction, deepens hypnosis appropriately, and then takes client to her safe place. With the mention of several feelings the hypnotherapist has some options in building the affect bridge.

Hypnotherapist: Breathe the sensations of your safe and special place into your being. Saturate every cell, every molecule, every atom with the good, positive, healthy sensations of hypnotic peace. In a moment I'll count from 5 to 1 and as I do your subconscious mind will take you back in time, back in time to an earlier time when you were active, and happy, and using your body. 5, beginning to move back in time now, 4, to a time when you're active, happy, using your body, 3, at the count of 1 you'll be there, 2, going back now, and 1, be there now, tell me what's happening, indoors or out?

This step is done prior to the affect bridge to demonstrate to the client in a non-threatening way that they can travel back in time.

Client: I'm outside. I'm in the park, playing tag with my friends.

H: How does it feel to be outside, playing tag with your friends?

C: Wonderful! I'm so strong and I have so much energy.

H: Good, breathe these wonderful sensations into your being.

Client is able to connect with her feelings in a pleasant situation which in turn helps to later create the affect bridge. This scene may also serve as a point of reference if necessary.

H: In a moment I'll count from 5 to 1 and your subconscious mind will take you to another active, happy time. *5 to 1 count, be there now . . .* what's happening?

C: I'm just little, I'm riding a big horsey, his name is Santana . . .

Reinforcing the positive connection of this second experience, the hypnotherapist then moves on.

H: In a moment I'm going to count from 5 to 1 and as I do your subconscious mind will take you back to a recent time in your life when you were feeling such a sense of devastation. Focus on the feeling of devastation now, and as I count, your subconscious mind takes you to a recent time where that devastation is so strong, so real . . . 5, going back now, 4, to an earlier scene, event or situation that has everything to do with this sense of devastation, 3, at the count of 1 you'll be there, 2, and 1, be there now, what's happening, indoors or out?

This step starts to move the client back in time toward their ISE. An SPE is relatively easy to access since it happened recently.

C: Indoors. I'm at the doctor's. He just told me I can't get pregnant. [Begins to cry.]

H: How does that make you feel?

C: I'm crushed, devastated. I feel like the bottom has dropped out of my stomach.

H: Are these feelings of being crushed, devastated, bottom dropping out of your stomach new to you or familiar?

Familiar feelings indicate we have not uncovered the ISE and must continue on. If the client responds with "new" we will then look at reframing the event. We will not do the transformational piece, or reframe the event, until we have reached the ISE.

C: Familiar.

H: Focus on these feelings now. In a moment I'm going to count from 5 to 1 and as I do, your subconscious mind takes you back to an earlier time, a time that has everything to do with these feelings of devastation, that sense of the bottom dropping out of your stomach. *5 to 1 count again, be there now . . .* What's happening, indoors or out?

C: Inside.

H: What's happening in this experience your mind has taken you to?

C: I'm lying in bed with my boyfriend. He just broke up with me. He knew he was going to do it but he slept with me anyway.

H: How does that make you feel?

C: I'm devastated. I feel sick to my stomach. It's like

55

my world is coming undone. I can't believe it, I thought we were so happy. [Abreaction.]

H: What age are you?

C: Twenty. I'm in college. He was my first real love. I thought he was. We were going to get married, have a family, and now it's just over, just like that, so cruel.

H: These feelings, of devastation, sick to your stomach . . . are they new or familiar?

C: Familiar.

H: Do you make any type of decision at this time?

C: You can't trust anyone, can't let anyone close to you. *Hmmm . . .*

H: All right, focus on these feelings again, that sense of devastation, that sick to your stomach feeling. In a moment I'll count from 5 to 1 and as I do, your subconscious mind takes you back in time, back to an earlier time, perhaps the very first scene, event or situation that has everything to do with this sense of devastation . . . 5, climb into these feelings now, 4, going back in time, 3, back to the very first scene, event or situation that has everything to do with these feelings, 2, and 1, be there now, what's happening in this place that your mind has taken you to?

C: I'm sitting on the ground. I'm crying. I fell off the monkey bars in the school yard. No, I was pushed off. That mean kid, Billy Brown, pushed me off. He's such a bully, he's always hurting somebody. I was going to win and then he pushed me.

H: You're on the ground crying, he pushed you off the monkey bars, how does that make you feel?

C: I'm mad and sad. My tummy hurts too.

As the client regresses in age it may become apparent in their choice of vocabulary. However, they usually maintain the ability to converse in adult terms as well.

H: Are these feelings new to you or familiar?

C: Familiar.

Once again we will move through time toward the initial sensitizing event. Occasionally the client will go straight to the ISE but not always. It is more likely that several subsequent sensitizing events (reinforcements of the ini-

tial event we are seeking) will be accessed prior to reaching the first event. It is important to note that we are concerned with the feelings rather than the specific event. It is possible and even probable that as we continue back in time the events accessed may seem less and less directly connected to the issue. It is important to remember that the subconscious mind does not adhere to the logic of the conscious mind.

H: Focus on these feelings . . . *5 to 1 count . . . be there now* . . . What's happening, indoors or out?

C: Inside. It's quiet. Dark.

H: Alone or with people?

C: Alone but I sense a presence.

Quiet, dark, alone but sensing a presence are clues that the client may be in utero.

H: What are you aware of?

C: Loss. A devastating loss. I feel sobbing.

H: Tell me about the sobbing.

C: I feel it but it's not me. I'm not sobbing but I feel it

in my being. I feel like I am a part of this sobbing.

H: How does that make you feel?

C: Devastated. It's haunting. My stomach hurts, feels like the bottom has dropped out of it.

H: Are these feelings new or familiar?

C: New. They're new. I haven't felt anything like this before. It's terrible. I want to make it stop.

We have reached the original event, that is, the ISE. We'll need a little more information before we proceed to the transformational piece.

H: How can you make it stop?

C: I don't know.

H: In the hypnotic state you have access to lots of interesting tools. Become aware that you can get more information on this experience simply by intending to do so. Just as you can adjust a VCR or DVD player with a remote control, you can adjust this scene in the same way. You can rewind, fast forward, turn the volume up or down, whatever you need to do. Go ahead and make the adjustments you need to gain the information and when you've done that let me know by moving your finger.

Ideomotor response (finger signals) is a useful tool for the hypnotherapist in communicating with clients while they are in trace and the subconscious mind is at the forefront.

C: Client lifts finger.

H: What's happening?

C: I can hear better now. I'm inside my mom. It's my mom sobbing. My dad hit her, he hurt her real bad. She's scared. She doesn't know what to do. It's not safe. It's not safe to be pregnant. He could hurt the baby. She should have been more careful. She's blaming herself but she didn't know he would do this.

H: What can you do to make this better? Would you like to bring in your adult self?

Sometimes the incident will resolve itself with the client's realization of what occurred. Other possible resolution techniques include bringing in the client's adult self (who contributes adult knowledge, wisdom and experience to the situation), gestalt-type dialoguing techniques, (where the client has a discussion with an essential element of the experience such as an aborted fetus, an abusive parent, or even God), verbalizing, reframing, etc. The subconscious mind cannot distinguish between "reality" and "imagination" therefore the transformational hypnotherapy piece, which changes the effect of the experience at the subconscious level, is extremely powerful in the completion of releasing subconscious blocks. The client may have an idea about ways to "rewrite" the scene or the hypnotherapist may make some suggestions.

C: Yes. Adult me comes into the room and comforts mom. She (client's adult self) tells mom that everything is okay and that help is available. She calls the police and they arrest my dad and put him in jail. Mom feels better and now she knows it is safe to be pregnant because she's not alone.

H: What do you know about it being safe to be pregnant?

C: I know it's safe too! It's okay because I have the resources to have a healthy pregnancy.

H: Is there anything else you need to do with this scene?

C: No, it's okay now.

At this point we return to present time stopping at each SSE along the way and reframing as we go. Oftentimes the SSE's are already adjusted in the subconscious based on the reframe of the initial sensitizing event.

H: All right, in a moment I'll count from 1 to 3 and on the count of 3 you'll be at the playground scene with Billy, 1, coming forward now, 2, and 3, be there now . . . what's happening?

C: Billy tried to push me off the monkey bars but I knew he was going to try it and I was too smart for him. He fell down trying to push me and he's crying. Now the principal is coming and taking Billy into the school. The principal knows what he was up to and he's gonna get in trouble.

H: But you're okay?

C: I'm okay, 'cause I trusted myself and I was careful.

H: Anything else you need to do here?

C: Nope.

H: Okay, *1 to 3 count forward to next SSE* what's happening?

C: I just broke up with my boyfriend.

H: How do you feel?

C: Great. I've known for awhile that he's not what he seems to be and I certainly don't want to spend my life with him.

H: What happened?

C: I just told him it wasn't meant to be.

H: How does that make you feel?

C: Glad that I didn't waste my time with him. I'm proud of myself.

H: Anything else you need to do here?

C: No, it's good.

H: *1 to 3 count to SPE* . . . What's happening?

C: I'm at the doctor's office. He just told me that my pregnancy test result is positive! I'm going to have a baby! My husband is so happy! We're both just thrilled!

I don't direct the reframe nor do I make judgment on it. In this case the client chose not to receive the infertility diagnosis at all, and instead receive positive pregnancy results. She could have chosen many different ways to reframe; she knows which one is right for her.

H: How do you feel?

C: Amazing! I knew I could do it, I knew I could have a baby.

From this point I will future pace the client (progress the client into the future) and have them report on what is happening. Had this client not been pregnant right away in her reframe she would likely experience it in her future pace.

H: *After making sure there is nothing else to do with this scene . . .* Take yourself forward in time now, a few weeks, a few months, even a year or so . . . what's happening?

C: I'm much further along in my pregnancy now, I have a round belly and I can feel the baby moving inside of me! It's almost time to give birth, I'm so excited!

H: Move further ahead, now, you've given birth to

your healthy baby . . .

C: It's a boy! I knew it would be. My husband has his arms around both of us and I'm holding my sweet, warm bundle!

H: Move further forward . . . what's happening?

C: My son is starting school, wow, I have 2 other children! I have 3 children!

H: Enjoy this scene, this experience of having your babies, your children. This experience is etched into the depths of your subconscious mind and you continue to reflect on it between now and the time you actually give birth to your babies. This experience has already occurred in your subconscious mind and now it is simply a matter of time for your body to catch up. You know you can have a baby, you've experienced it. From this moment on you remain calm and relaxed, allowing your baby to come to you in its own time. In a moment I'll count from 1 to 5 and at the count of 5 you'll emerge from hypnosis feeling wonderful in every way. Knowing that each time you go into hypnosis you'll go in more easily, more deeply, more quickly, and that each time you work with the hypnotic state, whether you're here with me in this office, listening to a tape or CD, meditating, practicing yoga, or doing some form of self-hypnosis, you'll receive more benefit.

In the above example it is apparent that not all reinforcing events, or SSE's, were logically connected to the infertility diagnosis. However, the feeling connection is quite clear. Just as the anxious feelings created in a premature baby fed with tubes, reinforced during a childhood experience where Mommy had to be away for a couple of weeks, compounded by a car accident, results in a client's fear of elevators, (no elevator specific initial or subsequent events) or a person with fear of flying (SPE) may have SSE's that include falling off a roof, falling out of a wagon, C-section birth of self, etc., the fertility client may have (apparently) sexually or pregnancy related subconscious events or not. It's how the subconscious mind interpreted the experiences and subsequently strung them together that counts. In our example: The client's feelings caused by physical and emotional trauma to her mother when the client is in utero is then reinforced by the client being pushed off monkey bars in the school yard by a bully. These feelings are again compounded when she is dumped by an insensitive boyfriend resulting in a decision to not trust anyone. The protective subconscious mind responds by blocking conception, resulting in the infertility diagnosis.

An excellent resource for further information on hyp-

notic regression is The Power of the Past *by Drake Eastburn. You may visit Drake's web site at: www.hypnodenver.com.*

Case Study:

Josie had been through eight IUI's in about as many months. She had been diagnosed with "unexplained infertility." She was 28 years old. She and her husband had decided to try one more IUI. She hoped the hypnosis would help her be successful this time. She came in for her first appointment just a few days before the insemination would take place. I would have preferred to have more time to work with Josie but I didn't. I'd just have to make the best of the one session I was going to have time to do with her.

During her intake I discovered that Josie had been raped in college. It had been a date rape and no one had believed her. The rapist had gotten away with what he had done, and Josie had berated herself constantly for having been so stupid in the first place. I did a regression with Josie to address the rape. Because of the nature of the subconscious mind, the details of the experience are really not important. What is important is the mind's perception of what happened.

Josie thought she had already processed the rape, but upon regression, she discovered that not only had she not processed it, she had been continually punishing herself for it. She had decided that she was not sexually responsible since she had let such a terrible thing happen, and had, in effect, imposed a "lock down" on her reproductive system to punish herself for her carelessness. After hypnotically reframing the incident, Josie was able to show herself some compassion and kindness. The rapist was appropriately dealt with (subconsciously) and Josie was finally able to release the whole frightening experience. Josie called a few weeks later to tell us her IUI had been successful.

"I still see a lot of girls not claiming their power. Just sort of letting other people tell them what to do, and that's a learning process, like it was for me."

— Joan Jett

Chapter 9
Change Your Mind
Change Your Life

"Infinite patience produces immediate results."
— A Course in Miracles

Stress is a major culprit in health issues, and fertility is no exception. Often what occurs is what I describe as the switch to the autonomic nervous system getting stuck. Imagine a cat, minding its own business, sitting in the garden. Suddenly the cat sees a vicious dog lunging toward it and instantaneously the cat has its hackles up, is hissing, spitting, and takes off up into a tree. What has happened is the cat's sympathetic nervous system has been triggered: fight or flight response. As soon as the danger is over the cat sprawls out in the grass, licking its fur or taking a nap. The parasympathetic nervous system has taken over, allowing the cat to rejuvenate its energy. Unfortunately with people, it seems we often get stuck in that fight or flight mode where stressor hormones are continually released into our systems and energy is directed away from systems not deemed necessary for fight or flight — the reproductive system being one of them.

In his book *Boundless Energy* Dr. Deepak Chopra discusses the body's internal pharmacy and the mind/body connection. He says that the mind/body phenomenon is so obvious that he finds it amazing that modern medicine has overlooked it to a great extent. He talks about how the important role of neurochemicals and neuropeptides in physiology is finally beginning to be understood and how these substances are brought into being whenever you have a thought or emotion, circulating throughout the body and adhering to every organ system. The must-see movie, *What The Bleep Do We Know?!* illustrates this brilliantly, and is supported by its featured contributors, many of whom are highly regarded scientists, teachers, and authors.

Dr. Chopra cites endorphins as one example of literally thousands of naturally occurring biochemicals that the brain produces in order to create health and healing. He tells us there is a great advantage to these natural, internally produced chemicals over drugs that can be bought in a pharmacy, and that advantage is that our own neurochemicals are produced in just the right amounts, at just the right time, in response to the body's perception of pain or some other biological need. Dr. Chopra says that because they are part of the body's own natural healing system, there are no side effects to these natural biochemicals.

Explaining that just as the brain's natural pharmacy contains potent painkillers, it also contains compounds to reestablish balance in all the body's major systems, Dr. Chopra suggests that learning how to properly use the brain's pharmacy is literally the key to perfect health, and that by gaining mastery in this area, we are able to produce compounds that enhance our body's vital systems more effectively than any pep pill or stimulant could. According to Dr. Chopra, we are able to shut down production of any neurochemicals that weaken the body's energy-producing and healing capabilities.

Because the brain's neurochemical production is

controlled by the mind, Dr. Chopra says that the balance of mind will produce balance of the brain's chemistry, which will in turn promote optimum functioning of the body's energy systems. To create balance of mind, Dr. Chopra promotes the reduction and elimination of stress.

Many couples have lost faith in the natural process of conception and maintain too strong a conviction in the need for medical assistance. With more and more women in high stress jobs it's really no wonder that conception doesn't always occur immediately (disastrous in our want-it-right-now society) and "trying" to get pregnant is simply anti-hypnotic. The word "try" implies failure to the subconscious mind. It is another of those words you'll want to strike from your vocabulary. Replace try with an action word of your choice: I am *playing* at becoming pregnant; *loving; allowing; accepting*; etc. Hypnotherapy reduces stress and increases confidence, instilling a sense of control, which, in turn, enables you to maximize your chances of conceiving naturally and/or increases the success of medical assistance.

Approximately twenty per cent of women diagnosed with infertility issues are diagnosed with unexplained infertility. I believe the word "unexplained" is accurate from a conventional medicine standpoint, however, from a hypnotic standpoint I don't believe it is "unexplained" at all. In his book *There's a Spiritual Solution to Every Problem*, and in many of his lectures, Dr. Wayne Dyer has quoted Dr. Deepak Chopra's *"Happy thoughts create happy molecules, and healthy thoughts create healthy molecules,"* and other similar sayings. As there are numerous books focusing specifically on mind/body medicine I will leave it to you to explore these areas.

* * * * *

It is essential that you familiarize yourself now with the universal laws of the mind. These hypnotic laws have been taught to HypnoBirthing® couples for years, and versions of them are found throughout recent and centuries old literature.

#1: The mind can only hold one thought at a time. Opposing thoughts cannot be held simultaneously; therefore, affirming positive thought creates a positive outcome. Only the person thinking the thought has any say over what the nature of the thought will be. Only you can and must choose your thought. *HypnoFertility™ Application: You are responsible for the thoughts you hold in your mind – the cancel technique is an effective method of releasing the unwanted advice or projections of others, followed by positive thought such as* I embrace a healthy, peaceful pregnancy. *It is essential that you leave all negative thoughts behind and not bring that negative energy into the present. DON'T GO THERE!*

#2: Thought precedes reality. Whatever you focus on (internal or external in origin) becomes manifested. Intention creates experience. What you think (say) is what you get. Mental images become imprinted, and the subconscious mind plays out the plan. By imprinting positive plans through hypnosis and positive reinforcement, positive outcomes are realized. *HypnoFertility™ Application: Refusing to entertain negative thinking – regardless of what others think or say – and focusing on positive thought and action allows nature to take its course.*

#3: For every thought or emotion there is a related physical response. Thoughts that are imprinted into the subconscious create a biochemical response within the body; hence, over a period of time we can create our own health or illnesses with conditioned responses. *The rich get richer; the poor get poorer.* When fear is present the fight or flight response is triggered causing a flood of stressor hormones to be released throughout the body. Not helpful to a calm, relaxed state of mind conducive to conception.

HypnoFertility™ Application: Reinforcement of "I'll never have a baby" and other negative thinking patterns results in continual stress and triggering of the fight or flight response, causing chemical reaction and the body to actually fight itself. The use of hypnosis, meditation, and other forms of relaxation kicks in the parasympathetic nervous system creating an overall state of calm.

#4: New programming in the subconscious is always more powerful and always wins out over past programming when the two are in conflict. The non-reasoning, childlike subconscious cannot distinguish between fact and fantasy. If the illusion is that the new information introduced into the scene is for the person's well-being, the subconscious accepts the new programming — right or wrong. *HypnoFertility™ Application: This is beneficial when utilizing hypnosis for fertility as subconscious blocks are released and the belief that pregnancy is possible becomes truth. However, the natural knowing that the body can become pregnant can be destroyed by information (true or not) to the contrary received from any number of sources. The aura of authority and infallibility of medical personnel, the internet, or television can lead a vulnerable person to accept intervention contrary to her best interest. Application of the cancel technique is paramount in such situations.*

#5: Once a thought is accepted and acted upon, behavior becomes easier with each subsequent similar thought. Continued reinforcement of a thought or action tends to make the thought more readily accepted, and it becomes easier for additional suggestion of the same nature to be accepted and acted upon. Once a woman becomes aware that being calm, focused, and relaxed is possible, she more readily accepts this principle and acts accordingly. The conviction becomes stronger with practice. *HypnoFertility™ Application: Once a calm, relaxed state has been accessed in hypnosis, the mind realizes that it is not necessary to be uptight during the fertility process. The more reinforcement in the form of subsequent hypnosis sessions, self-hypnosis, meditation, yoga, hypnosis CD's, etc., the more and more natural the state of relaxation becomes and the easier it is to counter stress.*

#6: Once a thought is accepted by the subconscious, it remains intact until it is replaced by another. Regardless of information to the contrary, unless the original imprint is released and destroyed and a new imprint is substituted, a person will continue to harbor the original thought. If a woman has subconscious blocks of any nature (whether or not they are known) it is essential that they be removed in order to clear the way for the desired success. Hypnosis is the means of achieving this objective.

HypnoFertility™ Application: If the subconscious has perceived infertility as a form of protection or necessary punishment, pregnancy will not occur until that imprint has been removed and replaced by an acceptance of pregnancy or some similar positive perception. Hypnotic fear release and/or regression are typically necessary in these cases.

"Don't compromise yourself. You are all you've got."
– Janis Joplin

Laws of the mind and thought that effect change:

#1: Law of Desire: There must be a burning desire for the positive outcome. You must truly want the outcome you claim to seek. Secondary benefit derived from extra attention from family/friends, or a usual behavior of fragility, weakness, and needing help can create an obstacle to conception. Reinforcing belief in yourself as an independent individual can result in a far different outcome.

#2: Law of Harmonious Attraction: This is by far the most important law of thought; and, yet, it is one of the most difficult to apply. All that you say (or hear) and believe is what you get. We attract conditions and situations that are in harmony with our thinking. Like attracts like. It is essential that any situation that is not wanted be totally avoided. Leave all negativity to others — DON'T GO THERE!

#3: Law of Belief/Expectancy: Success is achieved only with your trust in yourself and the belief that it can be done. What one expects to happen, inevitably happens.

#4: Law of Relaxation: Also the law of opposite effort. If doing manual work, one must put all effort into it. When approaching mental work, one must step aside and let it come naturally. Desired outcomes cannot be forced or manipulated. Imagery is the tool; thought is the technique. Thoughts are things. Thoughts have energy that is the ability to bring about the desired change or circumstance.

#5: Law of Visualization: You must see the positive end result. "Think from the end," as Wayne Dyer teaches. Dr. Joe Dispenza is now famous for his reference to this type of thinking in the movie *What The Bleep Do We Know?!* Through hypnosis techniques you can be helped to see yourself clearly conceiving.

#6: Law of Substitution: Since the mind can hold only one thought at a time and you are the person who chooses what that thought will be, it is essential that negative thoughts be immediately canceled and that empty space be filled with a substituted positive imagery.

#7: Law of Mental Practice: Daily practice of hypnosis and other techniques such as meditation reinforces the balance of mind/body/spirit. Hypnotic suggestion becomes more powerful with repetition and the more you experience the state of relaxation the more natural it becomes for you.

#8 Law of Self-Concept: You must know that you are deserving and capable of achieving the desired outcome. You must know that you are a mature, decisive, independent, empowered woman who is able to think and choose for yourself. If you are constantly subjecting yourself to the negative thoughts of others you will continue to lose faith and trust in yourself, and your body's natural abilities. The negatives must be released and your strong sense of self-confidence must be at the forefront of your mind. This is your responsibility — no one can do it for you.

Chapter 10
Becoming The Author
Of Your Life Story

"The thing women have got to learn is that nobody gives you power. You just take it."

— *Roseanne*

Having given birth to my second child in 1995 utilizing hypnotic techniques, I am extremely supportive of the power of hypnosis in promoting calmness and comfort for mother, child and birthing companion during the birthing process. I can also speak firsthand about the power of hypnosis for fertility, having conceived my son utilizing some of these very techniques to overcome issues due to a vasectomy reversal which was only partially successful.

"Optimism goes all the way with pessimism but arrives at a point far beyond it." This philosophy is taught by my mentor, Dr. C. Scot Giles* to persons living with cancer as they progress toward health. The body has a natural tendency toward health and embracing an optimistic outlook supports this re-balancing. Hypnotism is the method of teaching this principle to the mind.

Hormonal problems often contribute to conception issues. Restoration of hormonal balance and eventual pregnancy may occur by utilization of these techniques and implementation of positive lifestyle changes such as diet and exercise. Hypnosis is well recognized for its effectiveness in smoking cessation, weight control, stress release, and general habit changing. Interestingly, these same issues pose the biggest threat to fertility.

The goal of my program is not simply for you to become pregnant, but rather is to enable you to attain personal empowerment. For only by doing so will you truly be able to let nature take its course. Through personal empowerment comes inner peace, the ability to accept, appreciate, and embrace life.

Case Study:

31-year-old Louise and her husband had been "trying" to have a baby for three years when she came to see me early in 2004. Though she'd had surgery to remove a benign fibroid tumor, her diagnosis was "unexplained infertility." Several medical procedures, including clomid and IUI's, had failed and her reproductive endocrinologist had recommended IVF. Afraid of the physical and emotional effects of IVF, Louise wanted to do hypnosis first.

Upon interviewing Louise, I discovered she'd had no previous pregnancies. She was happily married and enjoyed her work as a nurse. She was healthy, took good care of herself, exercised and ate well. She maintained a healthy weight and did not smoke. Louise had a good relationship with her parents and was herself a "wanted" child. Her parents were supportive of her. She'd had no physical, emotional or sexual abuse. Her own birth had been somewhat difficult and had resulted in an emergency c-section.

I suggested four hypnosis sessions at Louise's convenience because she wanted to conceive naturally and there was no time crunch or need to accommodate medical protocols.

Session #1

The hypnotic induction was followed by the creation of Louise's safe place. As Louise rested in her safe place, I reminded her subconscious mind that it knew how to become pregnant and that a healthy pregnancy was the goal. I guided her to the control room of her subconscious mind where she was able to make pregnancy-conducive adjustments to a control panel representing her body/mind/spirit. Louise reported that she made adjustments to several knobs, buttons and switches, though she was not consciously aware of why she felt guided to do so. She just knew she was supposed to.

When Louise was finished in her control room there was still quite a bit of time left so I guided her through a body scan. She found her uterus warm and inviting and met a little nurse there named Joy. Joy assured Louise that all was well and that she would soon be pregnant. Before ending her session Louise went forward in time and held her baby as tears of joy streamed down her face. Louise practiced her stress reduction CD daily until her next appointment one week later.

Session #2

At her next session Louise reported having more energy. She felt her attitude was better — more relaxed. She had checked in with Nurse Joy during her self-hypnosis practice and even found the little nurse to be more positive. She reported several vivid dreams of which she couldn't recall many details.

Louise was looking forward to accessing the hypnotic state and we got started after a brief check-in. After an interactive fear-release Louise touched base with Nurse Joy again. Finding everything in order she then felt the need to send the baby a personal invitation, welcoming the baby into her family. As Louise connected with her baby, I gave her positive confidence-reinforcing suggestions and reminded her subconscious that pregnancy was natural. In her future pacing she held and rocked her sweet little bundle. Less than a month later we received the call that Louise wouldn't be booking a third appointment right away — she was pregnant!

* *Dr. C. Scot Giles is the creator of the ICAN Program, a hospital based, medically approved program using hypnotism as an adjunct in the treatment of cancer. It is a cooperative venture of La Grange Memorial Hospital in La Grange, Illinois, and Dr. Giles, and was the first approved program of its kind in America. Patients have been helped since 1991 with*

spectacular results. Published outcomes research on this program show that participants have an average ten year survival that is better than the estimated five year survival for their cancer when compared to the national cancer outcomes database. To read Dr. Giles' research go to: www.ngh.net and click on downloads or visit his web site: www.csgiles.org.

Chapter 11
Truth Is Subjective

"Nothing exists except atoms and empty space; everything else is an opinion."

— *Democritus*

I have often heard people say that something is not effective because it can't be scientifically proven. This is especially true of medical professionals who are sometimes unsupportive of other less traditional modalities such as hypnosis. A number of holistic methods are being studied and research has shown the efficacy of hypnosis, acupuncture and other such techniques in numerous areas. Hypnosis was recognized by the AMA in 1958 and documented studies are available for review through numerous sources. Skeptics always have an answer to support their viewpoint and I find it fruitless to waste time and energy trying to convert them.

In answer to any challenges regarding the efficacy of hypnosis for infertility I have only this to say: it was once thought that the world was flat, that the earth was the center of the solar system, that people who didn't follow a particular religious practice should be hanged or burned at the stake. These mythological truths are no longer accepted in our society, and, in fact, anyone attempting to adhere to them would be laughed at if not locked up. Science may attempt to dismiss the success stories of my clients as "anecdotal evidence," however, many scientifically accepted beliefs are skewed—research is incomplete, follow-ups have not been done, research was funded by a non-neutral party, etc. Every one of my clients will tell you this: they would rather have their "anecdotal" babies than a clinically proven scientific study.

I have been asked whether I am doing my own research or scientific studies. My response has always been the same: due to the nature of hypnosis itself, I would be unable to accurately document my success. In order for a study to be accepted scientifically, it must meet certain criteria. I would have to taint my own methods in order to adhere to these rigid requirements. My methods are dependent on my rapport with each individual client, and I choose my techniques based on a combination of knowledge gleaned from intake, experience, and intuition. Not one session I have ever done is the same as any other one and even if I tried to duplicate one, it would be skewed by the fact that each client is different, and even if I read a script word for word there is always the possibility of an unintentional inflection or pause that would, in fact, contaminate the effect.

Interestingly the Mayo Clinic addressed this issue in exactly the same way in an article published on their web site. I am grateful for permission to reprint an excerpt from this article here:

Mayo Clin Proc. 2005;80(4):511-524

EVALUATION OF THE CLINICAL TRIALS

Evaluation of clinical trials of hypnosis is complicated by the nature of hypnosis. The gold standard of a randomized, double-blind, controlled trial is virtually impossible because cooperation and rapport between patient and therapist are needed to achieve a receptive trance state. The few hypnosis trials that were blinded involved suggestions delivered by audiotape during surgery while patients were under general anesthesia (assumed to be a hypnoticlike state). Evaluation of these trials is limited by the lack of standardized techniques for hypnotic induction, evaluation of the level of trance, delivery of suggestions, or number and length of sessions. Although the state of hypnosis involves increased receptivity to acceptable suggestions, the methods of delivering the suggestions vary substantially. In some trials, researchers gave suggestions only for relaxation or no suggestions at all. In other trials, researchers indirectly suggested that patients allow a feeling or imagination rather than directing them to have a certain feeling, which relied on patients understanding the intention. In some studies, researchers gave suggestions only to distract the mind during an otherwise uncomfortable procedure or condition.

Thus, it is reasonable to consider the appropriateness of judging hypnosis by the best or worst results, with use of averaging, or by meta-analyses. Indeed, although better methods would be expected to achieve better results, many trials gave too few details about technique to allow comparison. If the most efficacious hypnosis techniques were known, a more representative review of the state of the art may include only trials using such techniques.

90

A deficiency of the trials reviewed is the lack of randomization of patient and practitioner variables that may affect outcome. Patient characteristics such as fear, attentiveness, interest, expectation, suggestibility, motivation, desire, and belief in hypnosis may alter outcomes. According to the literature, vital practitioner characteristics include training and experience and the ability to induce trance, to properly word suggestions, and to establish the necessary states of expectancy, rapport, and motivation (if not already present).1,24,35 Furthermore, results from clinical trials may not accurately estimate the effectiveness achievable in an office setting with willing, expectant patients. In clinical trials, many patients are likely to be unwilling, unmotivated, or skeptical about hypnosis. Hypnosis appears to be "particularly useful and yields better results when it is specifically requested by the patient."16 Consequently, clinical trials may underestimate the benefits of hypnosis compared with those obtainable by a proficient, experienced hypnotist.

David R. Hawkins, M.D., author of the book *Power vs. Force* explains his personal experience as one in which subjective interpretation preceded the scientifically researched and objectively organized data which he presents as truth, thus suggesting that awareness is itself the inspiration for scientific veracity.

In a 1999 book called *Secret Formulas of the Wizard of Ads*, author Roy H. Williams wrote the following: *Although none of the neurologists I've consulted can positively confirm or deny it, I am convinced that while a speaker uses Broca to arrange his words into understandable sentences, the listener uses Broca to anticipate and discount the predictable. When your listener hears only what she has heard before, it's difficult to keep her attention . . . . When speaking or writing, visualize Broca's area as a theater stage upon which your play will be performed in the listener's mind, and think of Broca as a theater critic – the judge who will determine whether or not to walk out on your play. If you will present your play on this mental stage and gain the smiling approval of the judge, you must electrify Broca with the thrill of the unexpected.*

For more than four years Mr. Williams endured a great deal of criticism from people who were unable to find any "proof" of Broca's area of the brain anticipating the predictable. His response to their indignant e-mail demands for documentation was flimsy at best: "I've never read it. It was not taught to me. Can a man not speak the truth without quoting someone else?"

I speak the truth – I know it intuitively. Eventually someone will prove it scientifically, but that is not my concern. My clients want babies. The information in this chapter should shed some light on where I'm coming from. I have helped a lot of women become pregnant. It's not something I do or even something I take credit for. I am the facilitator. I help you get back on track, back in balance of mind, body and spirit. Hypnosis is the tool. The following chapters will continue to enlighten you with the power of hypnosis, the power of your own mind. Each and every one of my clients has told me, "I feel there is a baby there." I believe that. I believe you. I believe *in* you. The rest, as they say, is history. Or, in this case, *her*story. The babies don't care if you call them "anecdotal evidence." They're warm, and they're pink, and they have that heavenly smell . . .

Note: Chapter 20 of Roy Williams' book *Magical Worlds of the Wizard of Ads* bears the heading:

It's Party Time!

May the name of Peter Gorner live forever, Amen. On Monday, April 23, 2001 the Chicago Tribune *published a story about the brain that I had waited four long years to read. In that story, the* Tribune's *Pulitzer Prize-winning science reporter, Peter Gorner wrote:* A story published Sunday in the journal *Nature Neuroscience* suggests for the first time that the rules of music may be processed in the same region of the left hemisphere located just above the ear, called Broca's area, that handles speech and language syntax . . . . " *Music training is known to lead to enhanced verbal abilities and this may explain why," said psychologist Burkhard Maess, of the Max Planck Institute of Cognitive Science in Leipzig, Germany, who conducted the research.*

Congratulations, Roy!

Case Study:

Having been diagnosed with Polycystic Ovarian Syndrome and Amenorhea at the age of 14, Denise had been told she'd have a hard time becoming pregnant. Her mother, a very negative person, continued to reinforce that suggestion at every chance she got over the next several years. By the time Denise was ready to have a baby, the years of negative reinforcement had become deeply ingrained, and as a self-fulfilling prophecy, she found herself unable to conceive.

Session #1

Following the intake I hypnotized Denise and immediately addressed the years of accumulated fears and negative expectations. We began to transform her beliefs from the negative to the positive and to redirect her attention from her irregular menstrual cycles. In the enchanted castle, Denise soaked in the healing pool and connected with her Inner Goddess who shared a message of hope. She discovered upon visiting her uterus that it was warm and welcoming and ready to nurture her baby.

Session #2

Denise was using her stress reduction CD each night and sleeping better than she had in years. She was feeling much more positive about the prospect of becoming pregnant and had elected to distance herself from her mother's cynicism for the time being. After metaphorically snuggling Denise into a relaxing cloud, I utilized a time distortion technique to help her release the expectation of being unable to become pregnant imprinted first by the doctors and then reinforced by her mother. I then guided her through a fear release to address her numerous pregnancy fears, conscious or otherwise. In her future pace she held her baby and tears streamed down her face as she reported sitting on a porch with many grandchildren and great grandchildren around her.

Session #3

Denise became pregnant! It was less than two months after her first session and she and her husband planned to make the announcement to their families over Christmas. We completed a general hypnosis session for reinforcement of relaxation and release of fears, followed by a future pace to the grandchildren scene once again.

Session #4

Denise had been feeling very nauseous. She planned to do HypnoBirthing® *the Mongan Method* and was considering a home birth. After a rapid induction I used hypnotic suggestion to assist Denise in releasing the nausea. In trance Denise was able to connect with her baby and send her love. By the end of the session the nausea was gone and Denise was feeling much better. Seven months later she gave birth to a healthy girl through a HypnoBirthing® Home/Water Birth.

Chapter 12
Why Hypnosis? What Motivated Some Of The Greats?

"Cautious, careful people always casting about to preserve their reputation or social standards never can bring about reform. Those who are really in earnest are willing to be anything or nothing in the world's estimation, and publicly and privately, in season and out, avow their sympathies with despised ideas and their advocates, and bear the consequences."

— Susan B. Anthony

Milton Erickson (1902 -1980) may have done more than any other individual in the 20th century to change the way in which hypnotherapy is practiced. As a boy he suffered from polio so severely that a doctor once predicted imminent death. Erickson overheard this and his annoyance with the doctor seems to have helped him to survive the episode, though he remained physically weakened for much of his life, and had to spend periods of time in a wheelchair. Told he would never walk again, Erickson spent many hours concentrating his attention on achieving a flicker of movement in the muscles of his legs, and he was up on crutches within a year. The determination which was thus revealed in childhood drove him to accumulate degrees in medicine and psychology; he then became a psychiatrist, working first in a number of institutions and later as a professor of psychiatry. He was a fellow of many international professional bodies and was founding president of the American Society for Clinical Hypnosis.

Dave Elman was born May 6, 1900 in Park River, North Dakota and died on December 5, 1967. His interest in hypnosis was stimulated at an early age by his father who was an accomplished hypnotist. When Dave was 8 years old he began to realize the vast possibilities of hypnosis in the relief of pain. This occurred when his father was dying of cancer and a family friend — a well-known hypnotist with an enviable fame for performing outstanding feats — relieved the intractable pain quite rapidly with hypnosis. Dave saw his father wracked with the pain of terminal cancer, yet in just a few minutes of hypnotic treatment the moaning and groaning was silenced and the pain was relieved. Little Dave was permitted to visit and play with his dad. Elman never forgot that his father was given relief by a stage hypnotist after the doctors had said there was no way to relieve his suffering.

Perhaps the best-known hypnotist of our modern era, Dave Elman has written extensively about the importance of promoting positive expectations in clients so as to ensure positive outcomes. In particular he relates in his book *Hypnotherapy* how amazingly successful Dr. Henry Munro, a Midwestern physician practicing around the turn of the last century, was in preparing his patients for surgery by the use of hypnosis, not only to alleviate their stress, but also to provide them with confidence as to the outcome of their procedures and their ability to heal well and quickly.

According to Elman, Dr. Munro was especially concerned about the incidence of death resulting from anesthesia, and through the use of hypnosis was able to dramatically reduce the amount of anesthesia (ether, in those days) his patients required. This combination of low doses of ether, positive expectations, and stress reduction gave Dr. Munro an excellent record of successful surgeries, however, his innovative approach was largely ridiculed by his colleagues.

It was only when he happened to meet with the Mayo brothers (who would later found their world-famous clinic in Rochester, MN) that he found a receptive audience for his new approach to anesthesia and surgery. The brothers agreed to see if they could duplicate Dr. Munro's methods, and what they achieved was phenomenal. Although it was not widely known that the Mayo brothers were using hypnotic methods, their many successful surgeries brought them new patients from all over the world.

Although initially drawn to hypnosis for personal reasons, both Elman and Erickson eventually devoted most of their lives to the advancement of hypnosis. Many articles and books have been written about these unprecedented individuals, and the only book Elman ever wrote, *Hypnotherapy,* is used in hypnotherapy trainings and schools almost universally. In 1958 hypnosis was recognized by the American Medical Association as a legitimate, safe approach to medical and psychological problems. Today more people recognize that the mind and body interact. Mind and body are integrated parts of a whole being; a change in one part affects the other.

Case Study:

Having seen the Denver 7 News report featuring my hypnosis for fertility work, Cheryl called my office long before we opened for business the next day. Upon reaching my office manager, Cheryl begged her to schedule an appointment with me as soon as possible, recounting a devastating personal tragedy. Diagnosed with cervical carcinoma II, 37-year-old Cheryl had only a few months in which to conceive and give birth before she would have to undergo a radical hysterectomy.

Within the week Cheryl was in my office. Having already undergone two surgeries, she had a lot of stress in her life, but none compared to the pressure created by a serious time-crunch in which she had to get pregnant if she were to *ever* have a baby of her own. Due to the circumstances, I recommended 4 sessions in close succession, however, extremely focused on finances, Cheryl opted to start with a single session. She was also considering IVF, however it was against her religious beliefs and again she was concerned with the expense. As always, I deal with what emerges — I put my focus on what I could best do to assist Cheryl in becoming pregnant naturally.

Much of the session was spent on the intake, through

which I gleaned the necessary information to create Cheryl's session. Beginning with a general induction, I assisted Cheryl in achieving deep hypnotic relaxation. She did a body scan, checking in with her surgery area and reporting it had healed nicely. She checked on her uterus which she found to be warm and welcoming for her baby; then accessed her control room where she made the necessary adjustments which would enable her to become pregnant. Meeting her assistant, she discovered a grandmotherly angel with strong nursing skills who would assist her through the process of conception, pregnancy, birth, and recovery. Her future pace revealed the birth of a healthy baby. Less than one year from that single appointment in my office, Cheryl gave birth to a healthy baby.

Chapter 13
What's Religion Got To Do With It?

"We need to find God, and he cannot be found in noise and restlessness. God is the friend of silence. See how nature – trees, flowers, grass – grows in silence; see the stars, the moon and the sun, how they move in silence . . . We need silence to be able to touch souls."

— *Mother Teresa*

The Catholic Church vehemently disagrees with the practice of IVF. The Mormon Church leaves it up to the individuals concerned. Many religions have opinions about a number of different issues and readers may or may not agree with any given stance. This is not about religious debate, however, this is vital information that I feel would be a disservice to omit from this work. For example, even if a woman considers herself a non-practicing Catholic, just the knowledge that the church disapproves of IVF can still be enough to create subconscious blocks to fertility. Remember that the first information received by our subconscious minds is accepted as truth, and our religious training often qualifies as one of our first sources of information. Even if we have consciously decided to choose another spiritual direction, if we have not released those initial ideas, we can become conflicted, whether we are aware of it or not.

I make no judgments about my clients' spiritual beliefs. I am simply aware that conflict is possible. I adjust my hypnotic work accordingly, based on information provided during the interview. Sometimes my clients are comfortable with their religious beliefs, and are relieved to finally be able to admit to themselves that they are uncomfortable with what they consider to be invasive medical procedures such as IVF. Sometimes a client desires to change her subconscious belief to one more in harmony with her current practices.

I support my clients in their choices and encourage them to keep their personal beliefs to themselves. I discourage infertility chat rooms and message boards as they are anti-hypnotic due to clients vicariously re-experiencing failed procedure after failed procedure. I have heard arguments to the contrary, citing issues of needed support or that there are sometimes positive experiences as well. However, with what you now know about the subconscious mind, I'm sure you understand why I think repeating any negative experiences (whether or not they are your own) can create needless blocks to the goal of pregnancy.

It is crucial to remain silent about fertility experiences, even though it may be tempting to commiserate with others in similar circumstances or even feel necessary to share with friends or family.

In *Manifest Your Destiny* Wayne Dyer's fourth principle is *You Can Attract to Yourself What You Desire.* He addresses the *Value of Secrecy,* telling us that when we speak to others about our efforts to manifest, our power is weakened. Dr. Dyer makes the point that in general, when we describe our activities to others it is because the ego has entered the picture, and this kind of approach considerably dissipates our power of attraction. Although it is human nature to talk to others about problems we want to alleviate (or at least are hoping that by sharing we'll be able to relieve some of their pressure) when we articulate our power to attract something, our attention shifts to the reactions of those in whom we are confiding. Energy is then dispersed in the direction of their reactions in the same way that it is when we share problems, rather than directed toward manifesting our goals. The moment a thought is presented to another, Dr. Dyer says, it is weakened. He urges us to, "Maintain privacy concerning your own unique, possibly mysterious-to-others, powers to attract to you what you desire."

In *Some Ideas for Putting this Principle to Work* Dr. Dyer suggests keeping your mental picturing to yourself, so that what you want to attract is a private matter between you and God; that discussing it with others will dissipate the energy in the direction of ego and the opinions of others.

In his newest book *Inspiration* Dr. Dyer reinforces the wisdom he has shared with us many times over the past 3 decades, listing what he calls *6 principles for living an inspired life.* I highly recommend the book as a powerful reinforcement to your new way of thinking.

Some of the principles he encourages us to practice include:

- Being independent of the good opinion of others.
- Being willing to accept the disapproval of others.
- Staying detached from outcomes.
- Remembering that our desires won't arrive by our schedule.

Again, these are guidelines presented for your consideration. They are in harmony with the hypnotic principles and laws of the mind mentioned earlier in this book. The more we reinforce positive thinking in our lives, the stronger the neural pathways we create, and the more natural it becomes for us.

Case Study:

Susan had been a hypnosis client of my husband's. He referred her to me when she disclosed some issues she was having with assisted reproductive technology (ART). She'd been diagnosed with "unexplained infertility" and had already done clomid for several months before beginning IUI's. She'd been through 8 unsuccessful IUI's and the doctors were recommending IVF, however her insurance would not cover it, and she had already had incredible strain on her body. Allergic to needles, Susan had experienced terrible reactions each time she was stuck with one. Her relationship was struggling and she had become obsessed with the whole thing. A practicing Catholic with strong beliefs, Susan quickly concluded that she was not on par with the whole IVF thing at all. She elected to focus on her body's natural ability to become pregnant.

Within one session, Susan reported that her cervical mucous had returned, also stating that she hadn't realized it was actually missing though she hadn't had any for approximately 12 years. She'd wondered about it but had been unable to get a definite answer to any inquiries she'd made to medical professionals about it and so had not pressed it.

The hypnosis sessions with Susan initially focused on rebuilding her confidence which had been badly shaken by so many invasive procedures. She was thrilled to feel as though she had "returned to normal" in her thinking patterns — no longer obsessed with pregnancy thoughts every moment of the day. In one of my treatment rooms which we affectionately call *the Womb Room* Susan curled up in the beanbag chair and I regressed her to her own conception. A powerful process for anyone, clients dealing with fertility issues are particularly impacted by the experience: curled comfortably in the fetal position, a blanket tucked snugly around their bodies, relaxing to the sounds of the surf, dolphins, a human heartbeat, the eternal "om" and the melodic sounds of hypnotic patter combining to create a sense of overall peace, joy, and love. Regaining her sense of self, Susan is confident in her ability to conceive naturally.

To date, I have worked with Susan 4 times. At press time she is enjoying a natural approach to becoming pregnant and is happy to report she is no longer obsessed with it. She practices her CDs regularly and is enjoying the time with her husband. Her future pace revealed a baby boy to her, and she confidently awaits his arrival.

A wonderful healing process I offer is a hypnotherapy session which takes place in an office we have designated for fertility. It's decorated in rich burgundies and soft blues, and pictures of angels and babies adorn the walls. You are supported in the fetal position by an oversized bean bag, tucked in with a soft blanket. (The process is powerful for couples also.) This is an excellent place for a regression, hypnotic rebirthing, or to relax while accompanied by the sounds of Dolphin Dreams. *Many years ago I became aware that I was to have another baby. Even before my husband had undergone the vasovasostomy necessary for this to be possible, I came across a phenomenal CD while visiting MarineLand® in Niagara Falls, Canada. As I purchased the CD I knew that eventually it would play a part in the birth of my second child. A few years later, it did. As an interesting "coincidence" the creator of that CD resides in Boulder, CO. I had no idea living in Kitchener, Ontario in 1992 that I would ever end up living in Colorado. Yet, years later, shortly after moving to Colorado, I met a wonderful woman and gifted psychic and astrologer named Karen, who is now a good friend of mine. Interestingly, she is the inspiration for* Dolphin Dreams, *her former husband, Jonathan Goldman*, recorded it when they were pregnant with their son, Josh.*

*You can find Dolphin Dreams *or learn more about Jonathan Goldman at: www.healingsounds.com.*

Karen Anderson of Distant Star Astrology *is located in Nederland, CO. You may reach her at: (303)258-7258.*

Chapter 14
There Is Power In The Past

"Fall Seven times. Stand up Eight."

— *Japanese proverb*

She sat quietly coloring in her book, soothed by the silence of early morning. She treasured the sense of security suggested by the soft light; and the gift of gentleness she could almost touch. Carefully she applied color to the page, delighting in knowing she could choose what she liked; she could create beauty; she could enjoy peace.

Suddenly there was chaos. She watched detached – almost disinterested – as a little girl's body flew across the room and crashed into the wall above the bed. As though in slow motion, the scene unfolded: the little girl's body as it collapsed onto the neatly made bed; the tiny arm jamming into the space where the mattress met the wall. The blows that followed looked painful, though she was actually more concerned about the little girl's shame, as her clothing tore away beneath the pummeling strikes, exposing areas that should be private, should be respected.

Where that idea came from she didn't really know. Her ears hurt from all the shrieking and screaming. The little girl made hardly a sound beyond the wind being knocked brutally from her lungs, and an occasional gasp which might have been for air. She didn't usually make much sound until afterward, and then sometimes she hardly had the strength.

Time went by so fast when you were having fun with a friend, or maybe riding a roller coaster, or playing at the park. But at other times it was painfully slow. Times like this. She worried that someone would hear. She hated the looks they would give her, but before she could ponder this further she was distracted from her worries by a smell; familiar yet vague. She couldn't tell if she really smelled something, or if it was maybe something triggered by the throbbing in her head or the ringing in her ears. Some-

times that happened. You could think you actually smelled something, but it was really an extension of another sense, or some kind of projection caused perhaps by injury.

If she did in fact smell it, the smell was coppery, kind of faint, or maybe distant would be a better word. She was aware of warmth. She was warm – hot even – feverish. Time was playing tricks again. She heard another sound, closer than the others. Sobbing; heart-wrenching sobbing. She felt a slight stickiness, kind of out-of-sorts. The light faded; disappeared for awhile.

She was thinking again. Berating herself for wearing the little jumper, although it was her favorite. Pants were better, safer. Long pants, or at the very least, a pair of thick tights. At least there was a pretense of protection from the blows. They didn't help much but it was better than shorts or sundresses. She felt weak; drained. She dragged herself off the bed in the fading afternoon light and made her way across the room where she retrieved her coloring book from the floor, and carefully picked up her scattered crayons. She'd better tidy up; she'd better be good.

This type of childhood abuse is all too familiar in the lives of many of my fertility clients. As a hypnotherapist I often bear witness to this type of revisited experience and it unfolds in much the same manner, the descriptions as vivid as one would actually expect in "reality." Presented in the first-person perspective it provides invaluable insight into the possible subconscious patterns that could develop including what may seem to be illogical fears of quiet—an underlying sense of constant dread or "calm before the storm." I include the above piece so that you may have compassion and understanding for anyone who has ever lived this experience. Including yourself. Dr. Wayne Dyer promotes the release of your history in many of his written works and lectures. I agree with him completely. And I agree with Dr. Dyer that in order to release your history, you first must embrace it.

There is a fine line between having compassion for one's trauma and becoming or remaining the eternal victim. No one enjoys constantly dealing with the victim personality. We all know the type: they preface every encounter with their claim to misery. "I'm a victim of sexual abuse," "I'm the child of an alcoholic," "I had a bad childhood," etc. Wayne Dyer puts it well when he says, "Your biography becomes your biology." Refusal to let go of the past results in *dis*ease. Not to say that we can't have compassion for people, in fact, we should. However, there is a fine line between being supportive and being an enabler. When we enable someone we help keep them stuck in their problems. We can use our aware-ness of our own past experiences to help ourselves and others if we choose to. We've all had the experi-ence of picking up the phone to hear that all-too-familiar voice immediately start in on all that is nega-tive . . . and we've felt our natural energy drain in-stantly from our beings. Some of us have justified the pattern in ourselves by explaining our need to warn people of our shortcomings so they won't be disappointed in us. Some of us have been raised to think that the ever-sacrificing persona is to be re-vered — that martyrdom is a coveted practice. What-ever our justification — this is a pattern that must be broken. If we are unwilling to heal these issues we will be unable to achieve our goals whether fertil-ity, happiness, abundance or whatever.

Addressing these issues with hypnosis does not have to be a lengthy and/or messy process. Hypnosis dif-fers greatly from traditional forms of therapy, and clients are often pleasantly surprised at how much they can release in a relatively short amount of time. Hypnosis is considered rapid change therapy. It is solution focused and goal-oriented. It dovetails nicely with self-help work such as recommended by Wayne Dyer, Louise Hay, Deepak Chopra, Caroline Myss, Sylvia Browne, Tony Robbins, Dr. Phil and others. In fact, clients who have worked for years with some or all of the aforementioned self-help authors and speakers have reported amazing jumps to the next level after just a session or two of hypnosis.

Case Study:

40-year-old Michelle didn't know about my fertility hypnosis work when she was referred to me to deal with panic attacks. As we discussed her high levels of stress and anxiety it came to my attention that Michelle had been diagnosed with secondary infertility. She had recently suffered a miscarriage, and was having a hard time with stress and depression.

As I explained to Michelle how hypnosis could help with her panic attacks, I told her about the "domino effect" which basically means that as you address one issue with hypnosis it will often affect another and another like tipping dominoes. I elected to use a hypnotic regression in Michelle's second session, first having established a strong sense of safety and relaxation by having her create her safe place during her first session and two subsequent weeks of working with a stress reduction CD.

Michelle had experienced an abusive childhood and was currently having marital issues exacerbated by her emotional state of mind. She was overweight, eating poorly and hadn't been exercising though she wanted to. Although it seemed Michelle had a number of significant issues to deal with, she was surprised to find she could process them rather quickly. Her regression session enabled her to reframe some of the abusive childhood experiences, and though we worked together four times, she was pregnant by the third session. Because she hadn't quite resolved all of her anxiety, we continued the hypnosis for two more sessions after Michelle found out she was pregnant.

Session #3

Babies are sensitive to the feelings and experiences of their mothers from the moment of conception. After hypnotizing Michelle on her third session I spoke to the baby, assuring him that he was wanted and loved. I guided Michelle to check with her inner assistant who informed her that the baby was safely fastened into his car seat (in the uterine lining). She assured her son that even though she would be working through some painful feelings, those feelings had nothing to do with him and that he was truly loved. We continued to work on releasing any remaining anxiety and reinforcing mind/body health for Michelle and her baby. Michelle went to her control room where she made adjustments that balanced hormones and normalized her blood pressure.

Michelle decided to come in for a forth session to deal with some developments in another area of her life. Six months later she gave birth to her healthy son.

Case Study:

39-year-old Beth had been diagnosed with secondary infertility. She had been to a reproductive endocrinologist who had informed her that her levels of Follicle Stimulating Hormone (FSH) were too high, indicating poor egg quality. Although she had been scheduled for IVF, her doctor cancelled the procedure after the unexpected test results came back, telling her he would reconsider IVF if her FSH levels lowered, but not to count on it.

Beth decided to seek out hypnosis to try to lower her FSH which had more than tripled in the span of just a few months. Her goal was to normalize the hormone levels so the doctor would then attempt the IVF. Time was of the essence and we began immediately. I wanted to get four sessions in with Beth before she went back for subsequent testing.

During the first session I helped Beth access her control room and make adjustments to her hormone levels. She also went in and checked on her egg quality which she found to be quite good despite medical advice to the contrary. Beth selected a plump, healthy egg from her stash, reminding herself that she only needed one. It only takes one good egg to create a healthy baby. I reconnected Beth with a successful point of reference from her past. Because she'd already had a successful pregnancy I used hypnotic suggestion to remind her subconscious mind of her previous pregnancy, and reestablish the pregnancy goal. (This technique is also effective for women with primary infertility — we simply use a different success as a point of reference.) To achieve maximum hypnotic benefit in the shortest amount of time, I had Beth work with a stress reduction CD between sessions with me.

Abuse issues uncovered during the interview were released both with a standard fear release and hypnotic regression. On her first session I also had Beth do a set of drawings which gave me some specific insight into her subconscious state. I was pleased to find the overall state of her drawings to be pleasant, and it seemed we would have a positive outcome.

On the morning of her fourth session, Beth excitedly

told me her news: she was pregnant! Before she could even have her FSH retested, before the possibility of IVF could be revisited, Beth was naturally pregnant. A few months later Beth came in to learn HypnoBirthing® so she could have the satisfying natural birth experience she had always dreamed of. Her daughter was born in early 2004.

Case Study:

Although she did have one child, Maria had suffered with (secondary) infertility for the past nine years. This was her second marriage. She'd gone through a terrible break up with her first husband and although she desperately wanted another baby, she just couldn't get pregnant. Her current husband, Bill, accompanied her to her first session with me. Bill was enthusiastic about the hypnosis. The doctors had diagnosed Maria with "unexplained infertility" and Bill felt that hypnosis would be the key to unlock this mystery. After all, Maria had one son, and Bill had two children from a previous marriage. There was no physical reason they couldn't become pregnant—and they both desperately wanted another child.

During the course of the interview Maria told me of the severe abuse she had encountered at the hands of her ex-husband. She had endured it for a number of years, feeling trapped in the marriage for the sake of the child he constantly threatened. A hypnotic regression revealed the subconscious decision to never become pregnant again, designed to protect Maria and her first child from further harm. With both Maria and Bill in trance, I was able to help Maria reverse her decision. Bill was able to assure her safety at the subconscious level and they both experienced holding their baby in the future pace before the end of the session. Less than one month after that first and only session Maria called the office to tell us she was pregnant.

Chapter 15
Getting Back To Nature

"Nature Does Nothing Uselessly."

— *Aristotle*

In our modern times, anti-depressants are becoming commonplace. Depression is a household word and the average person has experimented with more than one anti-depressant and often combinations of them. Medical diagnoses may even be made based on a trial and error type method — the physician tries you on several medications and your diagnosis is obtained based on a positive response to a specific medication. The problem here is that the effects of anti-depressants are still unknown. Although approved by the FDA, if you look up Wellbutrin, for example, in the Physician's Desk Reference (PDR) you will find — among numerous side-effects and contraindications — that it states that the effects are unknown.

Anti-depressants are one area of concern. There is a powerful push to medicate the population — in other words we are discouraged from leaving well enough alone and encouraged to alter our genetic makeup at every opportunity. This trend is apparent in various areas of our lives. As we move further away from an active lifestyle and become more and more sedentary there are increased reports of depression, anxiety, personality disorders, attention deficit disorder, obesity, etc. We are convinced we need diet pills to control our weight; pills to shorten or alleviate our natural menstrual cycles; ovulation kits and medical work-ups to assist fertility; drugs to induce or speed up labor; additives, preservatives, sweeteners and colorings to entice our appetites; preventative surgeries including double mastectomies when family history or genetic testing indicates an increased risk of breast cancer . . . and on and on.

Childbirth, at one time accepted as a miracle of nature, is now very often considered to be an invasive medical procedure. C-sections are prominent, often scheduled purely for convenience. Pitocin, a synthetic form of the hormone Oxytocin, is a drug commonly used in hospitals to induce labor. Pitocin has been approved by the FDA for the *medical* induction of labor, however it has not been approved for the *elective* induction of labor. Interestingly, all information regarding Pitocin has been omitted from the Physician's Desk Reference (PDR). Available manufacturer's information regarding Pitocin states that there have been no adequate and well-controlled studies to determine the delayed, long-term effects of Oxytocin on pregnant women. Or on the neurologic, as well as general, development of children exposed to Oxytocin in utero or during lactation.

Dr. Jia Gottlieb*, M.D., a colleague of mine in Boulder, CO has dedicated his practice to the integration of eastern and western medicine. He has written many articles of interest including one about the dangers of unnecessary surgery, and is currently finishing his book detailing fascinating information from his years of study of the brain. Physicians such as Dr. Gottlieb make it possible for us to bypass the fear factor and make informed choices about our healthcare options.

If we do not learn from history it will repeat itself.

Draw your own conclusions based on the parallels between what has happened with childbirth and anti-depressants and what we are seeing now with "infertility." As always, I promote balance. I'm not promoting a particular opinion, but I am drawn to notice patterns, and I find these patterns worth noting.

Dr. Gottlieb's upcoming book Pleasure *will change forever how you experience one of life's most important and intimate feelings. To discover how to avoid the seductive pitfalls of false pleasures and find the genuine satisfaction that leads to bliss, ecstasy, and the ultimate pleasure, I highly recommend reading this book. To get your copy of* Pleasure *or to find out more about Dr. Gottlieb visit: www.jiamd.com.*

Chapter 16
Creating Your Reality

"I believe that imagination is stronger than knowledge –
myth is more potent than history – dreams are more power-
ful than fact – hope always triumphs over experience –
laughter is the cure for grief – love is stronger than death."
— Robert Fulghum

Everything, including a baby, starts with an idea.
We cannot create something unless we can first
imagine it. Ideas become reality once we energize
them; once we add emotional energy. Studies have
shown that the emotion accompanying an idea or
image causes an idea or image to realize itself – the
more emotion, the faster the idea becomes reality.

Throughout the pages of this book, I have referenced Dr. Wayne Dyer several times. I love to read spiritual and motivational types of books, and I have mentioned a number of them here. Wayne Dyer is my ultimate favorite, and I have spent many pleasant hours pouring over his works, watching him on P.B.S., and listening to him in my car. I often recommend his work to my clients as a supplement to the work we are doing with hypnosis. Dr. Dyer often talks about the right people and the right things showing up when we are aligned with Spirit. Interestingly, as I was in the midst of completing this book, Dr. Dyer's new book *Inspiration* found its way into my hands.

In *Inspiration* Dr. Dyer writes of his own personal hypnosis session where he regressed to a time before he entered this lifetime as Wayne Dyer. This took place so that he might have a conversation with God, and find out his purpose for this lifetime. He outlines his regression in the book, and recommends that his readers follow his example and find a way to have this experience themselves.

As a certified hypnotherapist, I have been facilitating this type of regression work for a number of years. As an empath, I have also become aware of a recent energetic shift. I decided to have Amber, a

128

hypnotherapist at my office, facilitate a life purpose regression for me. What I experienced was astounding. Due to all the "coincidences" aligning to guide me in this direction, I knew that the outline of my regression needed to appear in this book, since it does align with my experience. (Note: I have found that clients experience "the between" in various ways, yet there is consistently a sense of peace and love.)

Upon finding myself in "the between" as I like to call it, I became aware of that familiar yet incredible sense of peace and love. I didn't experience a "one-on-one" conversation with God, as Wayne Dyer did, however, I found myself in a "library" of sorts with many large, old books.

Amber: What's happening?

Lynsi: Waves of energy, huge power waves. It's gray, soft, peaceful, loving. Brilliant light. Oh! You can be there and here. You forget when you come here but you can be there and here. You are always connected. It's like a periscope on a submarine. You are actually underwater but you can pop up and see what's above. You can do that here too. There's no time. You can go anywhere, there is no particular order.

You don't have to go forward. You get healing here so you can just know.

A: What are you aware of?

L: Books, many, many books.

A: Are you aware of your purpose?

L: Recording, writing, teaching . . . rewriting . . . oh, show people they can overcome the past.

A: Is this your life purpose?

L: Partly. Goodness. I am a gift of goodness to my dad. He had a hard time. My grandfather was mean, violent. He left right after I came in; it was time for my dad to have goodness. I am good. I forgot when I came through. I remember now.

A: What's happening now?

L: My book! It's right here in the library. And so is *Inspiration*. It's shifting now. I'm in what seems like a different room. It's full of babies! Babies are a gift of goodness! Liam is there and he's holding a butterfly. I'm getting something: the consciousness has changed, some kind of lower energies or something.

There's not enough babies coming through. But they're there. They say they're always there but the alignment is off. That's why the moms always feel them — they are there! But out of alignment. The energy is off. Love them, always love them.

A: Anything else?

L: The gift of goodness. Babies are the gift of goodness. It's never too late to recognize the goodness. Anyone can choose.

A: Is there anything else you need to do with this scene?

L: One of the babies is placing itself in one of my clients. I'm watching it happen. An easy, gentle shift, and the baby is there.

Amber concluded the regression at this point. As she emerged me from the hypnotic state I was in awe of the feelings I'd experienced: the sense of goodness I'd remembered was palpable. I'd always known the babies were there, yet now I'd actually seen it. When I saw Liam (Amber's son and one of my fertility babies) showing me a butterfly, I knew that getting the book finished was priority, that in writing it, I truly was fulfilling my purpose.

Many babies have been born of this fertility hypnosis work. I humbly offer my gratitude to the Universe for the opportunity to facilitate some of this incredible work. I trust that the information, thoughts, references, and case studies here will serve to inspire you, and bring you hope.

Namasté.

About The Author

"I don't go by the rule book . . . I lead from the heart, not the head."

— *Princess Diana*

Lynsi Eastburn is a National Guild of Hypnotists Board Certified Hypnotherapist and Certified Instructor. She is a Certified HypnoBirthing® Childbirth Educator, specializing in Hypnotherapy for Fertility. Lynsi and her husband, Drake, run a full-time private practice and hypnotherapy training school with four Colorado locations, and are in the process of opening branches in New Mexico and

California. Lynsi has created a Center for Women's Wellness within the Eastburn Hypnotherapy Center where women have access to a number of professionals in complementary modalities including hypnotherapy, psychotherapy, acupuncture, nutritional counseling, and massage. Lynsi has developed several advanced certification programs including the *Certified HypnoBirthing® Fertility Therapist program* and the *Gestalt-based Hypnotherapy program.* She is co-owner and instructor of the Eastburn Institute of Hypnosis in Colorado and is a faculty member of the Leidecker Institute in Illinois and the HypnoBirthing® Institute in New Hampshire. Lynsi has been featured on *Denver 7 News, WB2 News,* on local radio stations, and in print media including the *Denver Post* and *Conceive Magazine.* She is a regular presenter at the *National Guild of Hypnotists Convention* in Marlborough, MA, the *HypnoBirthing® Conclave,* and through *Colorado Free University.* She has trained therapists in her *Certified HypnoBirthing® Fertility Therapist* methods internationally. Lynsi is president of the Denver NGH chapter meeting and was presented with the prestigious *Hypnosis Research Award* from the National Guild of Hypnotists and the *Education & Literature Award* from the HypnoBirthing® Institute in 2005 for her groundbreaking work in the field of hypnosis for fertility.

Originally from Toronto, Canada, Lynsi currently lives in Arvada, Colorado with her husband, Board Certified Hypnotherapist, Drake Eastburn, and her two sons, Kelly and Dylan Brûlé.

Watch for information on Lynsi's upcoming Fertility Hypnosis Retreats – benefit from a relaxing and peaceful couples' haven set in the majestic Rocky Mountains of Colorado and featuring the multifaceted HypnoFertility™ process.

You can become a Certified Hypnotherapist and HELP PEOPLE!

Professional hypnotism training provided by Drake & Lynsi Eastburn is available through the Eastburn Institute of Hypnosis. Choose from 2 formats designed with your success in mind: a four-month semestered program or a 9-day intensive. Approved by the State of Colorado and certified by the National Guild of Hypnotists. Contact us for a free information packet:

martie@hypnodenver.com
or call **303-424-2331**

To find out how to become a Certified HypnoBirthing® Fertility Therapist visit: **www.hypnofertility.com** or **www.hypnobirthing.com**.

Interested in becoming a Certified HypnoBirthing® Childbirth Educator (CHBE)? Contact the HypnoBirthing® Institute: **www.hypnobirthing.com**

New:

2 new CD packages available by Lynsi Eastburn:

The IVF Assistant **is a powerful 4-session HypnoFertility protocol created to complement the IVF process.**

Natural Conception **is a 4-session specialty collection designed to complement the natural fertility process.**

Each set: $63 + s/h

For more information on our services and products, visit:

www.hypnodenver.com
   or   **www.hypnofertility.com**

H dif 16, 10

Dr Giles. Calypross p 86

ISBN 142510240-9

9 781425 102401